"OPTIMIZATION TECHNIQUES"

Dr. Ramchandra Govind Pawar
B.Sc, M.C.A., L.L.B., D.C.L., M.P.M., M.A. (Eco), M.Com, Ph.D
Principal
SVPM's College of Commerce, Science and Computer Education
Malegaon, Tal – Baramati, Dist Pune
Maharashtra (India)

Preface

No one walks alone and when one is walking on the journey of life just where do you start to thank those that joined you, walked beside you, and helped you along the way.

Over the years, those that we have met and worked with have continuously urged us to write a book, to put our thoughts down on paper, and to share our insights together with the secrets to our continual, positive approach to life and all that life throws at us. So at last, here it is.

So, perhaps this book and it's pages will be seen as "thanks" to the tens of thousands of you who have helped make our life what is today.

This book is a core reference to the Java programming language. It covers the fundamentals of the language, it is not organized or written as a tutorial. Programming concepts are explained, along with details of the Java. Figures and illustrations clarify concepts that are difficult to grasp in words alone. Highlight boxes summarize the main features of Java for easy reference and review.

We are grateful to all those who have helped us directly and/or indirectly in preparing this edition. Firmly, we believe that there is always scope for improvement and accordingly we will look forward to receive suggestions for further enriching the quality of text.

About The Author

Dr. Ramchandra Govind Pawar is currently working as Principal at SVPM's College of Commerce, Science and Computer Education, Malegaon, Tal – Baramati, Dist Pune. He is having Twenty years of Teaching and Industry Experience. In his Eighteen years of teaching experience he has worked at various positions like Lecturer, Assistant Professor, Associate Professor, Professor, Dy. Director, Director and Principal. He has taught to the various courses like BCS, BBA, B.Com., MCA, MCS, MBA, MPM etc. He has taught the subject like MIS, AI, LAB, DBMS, DDBMS, SPM, Fundamentals of Computer, Business Data Processing etc. Apart from Teaching he is good administrator so currently working as Principal of Commerce College, before that he has worked as Director of Management Institute SIBACA, Lonavala and Dy. Director at Sinhgad Institute of Management, Vadgaon(bk) – Pune.

He is approved Guide for Savitribai Phule Pune University for the subject of Computer Management, as well as he is Ph. D. Guide for the subject of Management at Tilak Maharashtra vidypeeth, Pune. He is guide for Commuter Science at Mats University, Raipur, Chattisgadh.

Under his guidance one Student has completed his Ph. D. in Computer Science from Mats University, Raipur. He is currently guiding six students for Ph.D. at Savitribai Phule Pune University.

He has completed a research project of two Year duration funded by BCUD University of Pune entitled "A critical Study of Quality in Computer Educational Institutes under University of Pune".

He has written book on Database Management System for MCA, Published by Success Publication, Pune.

He has organized 18 National and International level seminars / Conferences under his direction as convener.

He has published 32 Papers at National and International Journals

He has Presented 28 Papers at National and International Conferences

He has worked as resource persons on various National and International level Seminars and Conferences in India and abroad.

Awards Received

- Distinguished Alumni Award of the year 2010 by Govt. College of Engineering Karad, Dist. – Satara.

- Best Teacher Award 2016 by International Association of Lions Club Pune and Ajinkya D Y Patil University, Pune.

- Academic Prize: Ranked First in M.Com degree at Dr. B.N.Purandare Arts, Smt S.G. Gupta Commerce & Science College Lonavala, Tal Maval, Dist Pune in Academic Year 2015-16 (Scored 83.88% Marks).

- He Ranked 10th in M.Com. at Savitribai Phule Pune University in Academic Year 2015-16.

- Ranked Third in M.A. (Economics) at Baburaoji Gholap College Sangvi, Pune in Academic Year 2012-13.

Contents

Chapter I
ASSIGNMENT PROBLEMS

Introduction

Assignment is a typically used optimization on technique practically useful in a situation where a certain number of tasks are required to be assigned to an **equal** number of facilities, on a **one to one basis**, so that resultant effectiveness is optimized.

e.g. -   Jobs to be assigned to machines or worker.

  -   Vehicles no routs etc.

Note: Assignment problem is a case of transportation problem where number of sources is equal to the number of destinations i.e. number of rows and columns are equal for given cost matrix.

e.g. Jobs	Machines			
	A	B	C	D
1	10	12	11	16
2	8	6	5	7
3	11	10	8	12
4	7	7	6	9

Hungarian Method of Solution:

This method is useful for a balanced (i.e. n x n) assignment problem where the objective is of minimization.

Step (i)   in the given (n x n) assignment table or matrix, subtract the smallest element or number in each route from every element in that row.

Step (ii)   Subtract then, the smallest element in each column from every element of that column so as to get reduced assignment matrix.

Step (i) and (ii) can be interchanged.

Step (iii)   Draw the minimum number of vertical and horizontal lines necessary to cover all the zeroes in the reduced matrix, by inspection.

Start with the row or column having maximum number of zeroes to draw the lines.

(a)   If the number of lines = number of rows / columns

It implies that the **solution is optimum then go to step (IV)**

(b)   If the number of lines is **less than** (i.e. number of columns or row)

It implies that the solution is **not optimum** it needs further improvement, then **go to Step (v)**

Step (IV) Make the assignment as follows

a) Check the rows successively. Mark a square ( ) around a single unmarked (i.e. free) zero in a **row** (if present) and cancel all the other zeroes in its **column.**

b) Check the column successively. Mark a square ( ) around a 'single unmarked zeroes' in a **column** (if present) and cancel all the zeroes in its **row.**

c) Repeat **step a)** and **step b)** until all the zeroes in the matrix are either marked with a ( ) or cancelled out.

- Now, the squared zeroes ( ) represents the assignment and if there is exactly one assignment in each row and column, it indicates an **optimum solution.**

- Consider then the corresponding elements in the original matrix to find out the optimum value of the pay-off (time, cost etc.)

Step (V) if the solution is not optimum, then –

a) Select the smallest element among all the uncovered elements of the reduced matrix.

b) **Subtract** it from all the uncovered element and **add** it to the elements at the **intersection of the lines**, **keeping** the **other elements unchanged**.

- Then go to step (iii) (draw lines) and repeat the procedure until the number of assignments (secured zeros ( )) is equal to the **number of rows or columns** i.e. **optimum solution is obtained.**

Examples:

Example 1- Consider a job which requires four activities – cutting, assembly, finishing and packaging. Four workers are employed who can do all these activities. The time required by each of them (in minutes) to perform each of the activities are as follows:

Activities	Workers			
	1	2	3	4
C	14	12	15	15
A	21	18	18	22
F	14	17	12	14
P	6	5	3	6

How should these activities be assigned to the worker so that the job is completed in minimum time?

Solution

1. Subtract the smallest element in each row from all the elements of that row. Thus we get

	1	2	3	4
C	2	0	3	3
A	3	0	0	4
F	2	5	0	2
P	3	2	0	3

2. Subtract the smallest element in each column from all the element of that column. Thus we get the reduced matrix as.

	1	2	3	4
C	0	0	3	1
A	1	0	0	2
F	0	5	0	0
P	1	2	0	1

(The second and third column remain unchanged as the smallest element is zero)

3. Draw the minimum number of lines to cover all the zeroes.

- Column 3 contains maximum number of zeroes.

- Hence draw the first line along column 3.

    Now, row 'C' and row 'F' contains **two** zero each therefore draw the second and third line along them.

- To cover remaining single zero at row 'A' draw the line along them. (row 'A' or column 2)

- Therefore we get reduced matrix as.

-

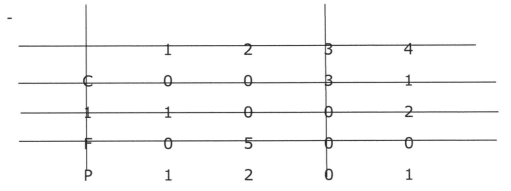

- Thus we need minimum 4 lines to cover all zeroes (which is equal to the number of rows) in the reduced matrix.

- Hence the solution is optimum and so **we make the assignment as follows**

4. Make Assignments :

a) (I) choose the **rows** successively. First there rows **have more than one** unmarked **zeroes** (i.e. zeroes without a( )or( )

Hence ignore them

But in the fourth row there is a single XXXX zero (i.e. at P_3)

- o Hence mark 4 with a ( ) and cancel all other zeroes in **its column 3** as shown.

(II) New **Proceed column wise**

First two columns have more than one unmarked zeroes. Hence neglect them. Third column has all the zeroes as marked.

(i.e. ( ) or) Hence neglect it. But fourth column has single unmarked zero in the third row at F_4

- o Hence mark it with a ( ) and cancel all other zeroes in row F (F3 already cancelled out.)

b) Repeat the steps (I) and (II)

Now again we go row wise as row (C) contain **two** unmarked zeroes neglect it.

But row (A) now contain **only one unmarked** zero at (A$_2$) (Zero at A$_3$ is cancelled already)

Hence mark XX with XX and cancel other zeroes in the **column2**

- Now proceeding column wise, we make last assignment at C$_1$ in column 1

So that all the zeros in the table is either marked ( ) or cancelled out

	1	2	3	4
C	0	0	3	1
A	1	0	~~0~~	2
F	0	5	~~0~~	0
P	1	2	[0]	1

Row-wise

	1	2	3	4
C	0	0	3	1
A	1	0	~~0~~	2
F	~~0~~	5	~~0~~	[0]
P	1	2	[0]	1

Column-wise

Again row wise and column wise assignment as follows

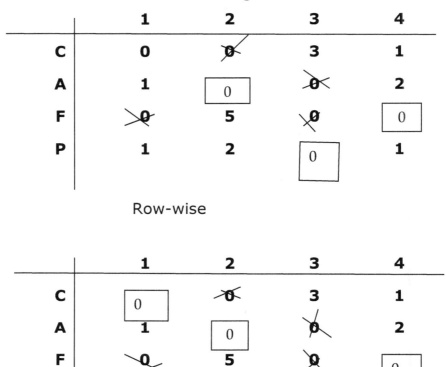

	1	2	3	4
C	0	0	3	1
A	1	0	0	2
F	0	5	0	0
P	1	2	0	1

Row-wise

	1	2	3	4
C	0	0	3	1
A	1	0	0	2
F	0	5	0	0
P	1	2	0	1

Column-wise

1. Zeroes marked with (0) represents assignment. As there is 4 assignment (which is equal number of rows / columns)

With each rows / column exactly one

Therefore the solution is optimum

Hence considering original table we have the optimum assignment plan as:

Activity	Worker	Time required
Cutting	1	14
Assembly	2	18
Finishing	3	14
Packaging	4	3
Total		**49 minutes (min)**

Example 2 :

Solve the following assignment problem for minimization

	1	2	3	4	5
A	8	8	8	11	12
B	4	5	6	3	4
C	12	11	10	9	8
D	18	21	18	17	15
E	10	11	10	8	12

Step (I)   subtract the smallest elements in each row

	1	2	3	4	5
A	0	0	0	3	4
B	1	2	3	0	1
C	4	3	2	1	0
D	3	6	3	2	0
E	2	3	2	0	4

Step (II)   subtract the smallest elements in each column

	1	2	3	4	5
A	0	0	0	3	4
B	1	2	3	0	1
C	4	3	2	1	0
D	3	6	3	2	0
E	2	3	2	0	4

Thus all the zeroes are covered using three lines which is less than number of rows / columns.

Hence the solution is **not optimum**

Step (III)

First improvement

i)   Select the **smallest element amongall the uncovered** elements. It is the element 1 (one)

ii)   **Subtract** it from all the **uncovered** element in the matrix and **add** it to the elements (3 & 4) at the **intersection** of the lines. Keep the other elements.

	1	2	3	4	5
A	0	0	0	4	5
B	0	1	2	0	1
C	3	2	1	1	0
D	2	5	2	2	0
E	1	2	1	0	4

Step (IV) Draw the minimum number of lines to cover zero.

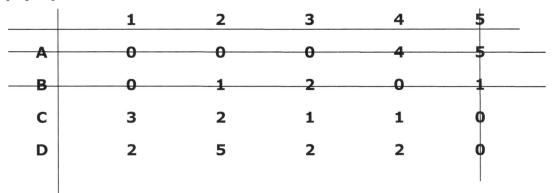

	1	2	3	4	5
A	0	0	0	4	5
B	0	1	2	0	1
C	3	2	1	1	0
D	2	5	2	2	0

| E | 1 | 2 | 1 | 0 | 4 |

Thus all the zeros are covered using 4 lines which is **less than** number of rows and columns.

Therefore repeat the step (iii) – First improvement again and then reduced matrix becomes

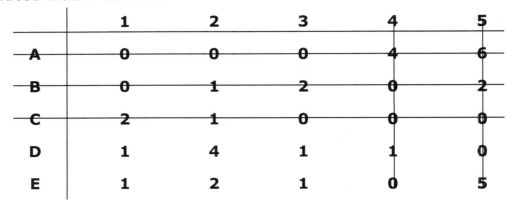

	1	2	3	4	5
A	0	0	0	4	6
B	0	1	2	0	2
C	2	1	0	0	0
D	1	4	1	1	0
E	1	2	1	0	5

Thus all the zeros are covered using **5 lines** which is **equal to** number of rows / columns

Therefore the solution is **optimum**

Step (V)   Make Assignment :
Proceed Row wise

	1	2	3	4	5
A	0	0	0	4	6
B	0	1	2	✗0	2
C	2	1	0	✗0	✗0
D	1	4	1	1	[0]
E	1	2	1	[0]	5

Proceed Column wise

	1	2	3	4	5
A	̶0̶	0	0	4	6
B	0	1	2	̶0̶	2
C	2	1	0	̶0̶	̶0̶
D	1	4	1	1	0
E	1	2	1	0	4

Step (VI) To get the optimum assignment. Policy as follows

A → 2

B → 1

C → 3

D → 5

E → 4

Hence by using original table we have

Minimum cost = 8+4+10+15+8

= **45**

Special cases in Assignment Problem

(A)   Unbalanced Problem :

- When number of rows is not equal to the number of column, it is unbalanced assignment problem.

- Hence we add the required number of dummy row or column with all its element a **0 (zero)** matrix, so as to make it a square matrix.

- Use Hungarian method to solve the problem four.

Example

Example (1)   The personnel manager of ABC company wants to assign Mr. X, Y and Z to the regional offices for which the costs are given. But the firm also has an opening in its Chennai office and would send one of them that branch if it is more economical than a move to Delhi, Mumbai or Kolkata.

Office/	D	M	K
X	1600	2000	2400
Y	1000	3200	2600
Z	1000	2000	4600

It will cost Rs.2000/- to relocate Mr. X to Chennai Rs.1, 600/-to relocate Mr. Y there and Rs.3, 000/- to move Mr. Z

What is the optimum assignment of personnel to the offices?

→ From the given information we can add fourth column corresponding to the **Chennai** office to the given cost matrix.

	D	M	K	C
X	1600	2000	2400	<u>2000</u>
Y	1000	3200	2600	1600
Z	1000	2000	4600	<u>3000</u>

Therefore it is unbalance type of cost matrix

Therefore to balance it we add dummy row with all its cost elements as '0'

Use Hungarian Method to solve the problem

Step (i)   Row Subtraction

	D	M	K	C
X	0	400	800	400
Y	0	2200	1600	600
Z	0	1000	3600	2000
Dummy	0	0	0	0

Since every column contains at least one element. Therefore Row subtraction is **same** as column subtraction

Step (ii)   Draw the minimum number of lines to cover all zero.

	D	M	K	C
X	0	400	800	400
Y	0	2200	1600	600
Z	0	1000	3600	2000
Dummy	0	0	0	0

This all zero's are covered using two lines which is less than number of rows / column.

Therefore, hence solution is **not optimum.**

Step (iii)   To make the solution optimum
           First improvement

	D	M	K	C
X	0	0	400	0
Y	0	1800	1200	200
Z	0	600	3200	1600
Dummy	400	0	0	0

Therefore number of lines < no. of rows/columns.

2nd Improvement

	D	M	K	C
~~X~~	~~200~~	~~0~~	~~400~~	~~0~~
~~Y~~	~~0~~	~~1600~~	~~1000~~	~~0~~
Z	0	400	3000	1200
~~Dummy~~	~~600~~	~~0~~	~~0~~	~~0~~

Therefore number of lines =4= no of rows / columns.

Hence the **solution is optimum.**

Step (IV) Make Assignment

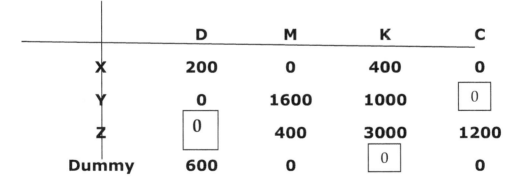

	D	M	K	C
X	200	0	400	0
Y	0	1600	1000	[0]
Z	[0]	400	3000	1200
Dummy	600	0	[0]	0

Thus the optimum policy is :

X → Mumbai

Y → Chennai

Z → Delhi

And Dummy → Kolkata   i.e. nobody is assignment to Kolkata.

Therefore Total minimum cost of assignment

=   2000+16000+1000

=   **4600/- Rs.**

Multiple optimum solution :

After making the assignments, it is found that two or more rows or columns still contain more than one unmarked zero's, then the problem has multiple optimum solution.

Example: Solve the following problems of assigning 4 co….. Programmer to 4 – application programmers, where estimated time in minutes required by each of them to develop the programmers is given.

Programmers	Programmers				
		1	**2**	**3**	**4**
	A	120	100	80	90
	B	80	90	110	70
	C	110	140	120	100

	D	90	90	80	90

Step (i)   Row Subtraction

	1	2	3	4
A	40	20	0	10
B	10	20	40	0
C	10	40	20	0
D	10	10	0	10

Column subtraction

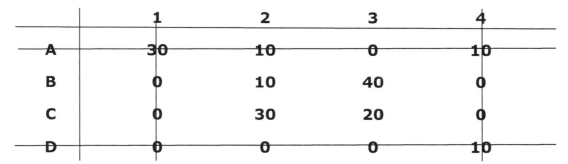

	1	2	3	4
A	30	10	0	10
B	0	10	40	0
C	0	30	20	0
D	0	0	0	10

Therefore number of lines required to cover all zeros = 4 = number of columns / rows.

Therefore, hence the solution is optimum.

Step (ii)   Make assignment

	1	2	3	4
A	30	10	[0]	10
B	0	10	40	0
C	0	30	20	0

D	**0**	0	**0**	**10**

Thus, the we can make the assignment A+ A3& D_2.   But rows **B and C** and column **1 and 4** still have two unmarked zeroes each. (Since we cannot make assignment further)

Thus the problem has **multiple optimum solutions**.

Therefore we can get the alternate solution as

i) All rows B & C, column 1 &4 have same i.e. **2** unmarked rows.

ii) Make assignment at B_1 and cancel all rows in its rows and columns.

iii) The remaining assignment is made C_4 which is single unmarked zeros.

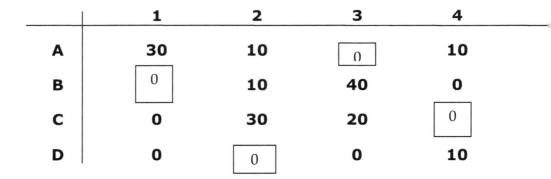

	1	2	3	4
A	30	10	0	10
B	0	10	40	0
C	0	30	20	0
D	0	0	0	10

Thus we have the optimum assignment as

A → 3, **B → 1**, **C → 4**, D → 2

And minimum Time   =   80+80+100+90

=   **350** minutes   (A)

If we make the assignment at B4 then

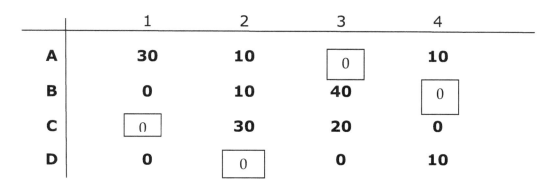

	1	2	3	4
A	30	10	0	10
B	0	10	40	0
C	0	30	20	0
D	0	0	0	10

Thus we have the optimum assignment as

A → 3, **B → 4, C → 1**, D → 2

And minimum time   =   80+70+110+90

                          =   **350** minutes   (B)

Hence from (A) & (B) XXXXXXXXXXXXXXX

Maximization problems

The Hungarian method for minimization problem can be used to solve the maximization problem as follows

i)   Convert the given profit matrix into a relative loss matrix, by **subtracting** all its elements from the **largest element** in it **(including itself)**

ii)   Solve further using Hungarian method to get optimum assignment.

iii)   To find the total maximum profit, considering the original profit elements for the respective assignment.

Example

Solve the following problem for maximizing the production output

Operators	Machines			
	A	B	C	D
1	10	5	7	8
2	11	4	9	10
3	8	4	9	7
4	7	5	6	7
5	8	9	7	5

Solution

The given problem is of **maximization** type and it **unbalanced** also. Hence add first **dummycolumn first** with elements '0' then convert production matrix into relative loss matrix by subtracting each in its

Elements from the largest element in it i.e. 11

Step (I)

	A	B	C	D	Dummy
1	10	5	7	8	0
2	11	4	9	10	0
3	8	4	9	7	0
4	7	5	6	4	0

| 5 | 8 | 9 | 7 | 5 | 0 |

Production profit matrix

	A	B	C	D	Dummy
1	1	6	4	3	11
2	0	7	2	1	11
3	3	7	2	4	11
4	4	6	5	7	11
5	3	2	4	6	11

Relative production loss matrix

Step (ii)

Further use Hungarian method

	A	B	C	D	Dummy
1	0	5	3	2	10
2	0	7	2	1	11
3	1	5	0	2	9
4	0	2	1	3	7
5	1	0	2	4	9

Row subtraction

	A	B	C	D	Dummy
1	0	5	3	1	3
2	0	7	2	0	4
3	1	5	0	1	2
4	0	2	1	2	0

5	1	0	2	3	2

Column subtraction

Therefore total number of lines required to cover all zero = number of row / column = 5

Therefore the solution is optimum

Step (iii)   Make assignment

	A	B	C	D	Dummy
1	0	5	3	1	3
2	0	7	2	0	4
3	1	5	0	1	2
4	0	2	1	2	0
5	1	0	2	3	2

Therefore using original production matrix

Operator	Machine	
1	A	10
2	B	9
3	C	9
4	D	10
5	Dummy	0

Alternate Solution

Example : Four different jobs can be done on four different machines. The setup and take down time costs are assumed to be prohibitively high to change out. The matrix below gives the cost in rupees of produce job 'i' on machine 'j' How should the jobs be assigned to the various machines so that the total cost is minimized.

Machines

	Machines			
Jobs	**M1**	**M2**	**M3**	**M4**
J1	5	7	11	6
J2	8	5	9	6
J3	4	7	10	7
J4	10	4	8	3

Step (i) a)   Row subtraction

	M1	M2	M3	M4
J1	0	2	6	1
J2	3	0	4	1
J3	0	3	6	3

J4	7	1	5	0

a) Column subtraction

	M1	M2	M3	M4
J1	0	2	2	1
J2	3	0	0	1
J3	0	3	2	3
J4	7	1	1	0

As (3 lines < number of rows / column =4)

Therefore there is not optimum solution

Therefore improvement by using smallest uncovered element 'I'

	M1	M2	M3	M4
J1	0	1	1	0
J2	4	0	0	1
J3	0	2	1	2
J4	8	1	1	0

Therefore select column wise: minimum number of line required to cover all zeroes.

Again solution is not optimum, since number of row = 3 < number of column / rows = XXXXX

Therefore, again **Improvement** by using smallest uncovered element = 1

	M1	M2	M3	M4
J1	0	0	0	0
J2	5	0	0	2
J3	0	1	0	2
J4	8	0	0	0

Therefore 4 lines are required to cover all zeroes = number of rows / column = 4

Therefore => The problem have multiple optimum solutions

(As all rows and columns have more than one single unmarked zeroes)

a) Select J1M1: 1st Solution.

	M1	M2	M3	M4
J1	[0]	0	0	0
J2	5	[0]	0	2
J3	0	1	[0]	2
J4	8	0	0	[0]

To get optimum assignment as

$J_1 \to M_1$, $J_2 \to M_2$, $J_3 \to M_3$ & $J_4 \to M_4$

Therefore, minimum cost = 5+5+10+3

= **23**

b) **Select : J1M2 → 2nd solution**

	M1	M2	M3	M4
J1	0	0	0	0
J2	5	0	0	2
J3	0	1	0	2
J4	8	0	0	0

Therefore optimum assignment as

$J_1 \to M_2$, $J_2 \to M_3$, $J3 \to M_3$ & $J4 \to M_4$

Therefore minimum cost = 4+7+9+4+3

= **23**

C) Then select $J_1 M_3$ 3rd solution

Minimum cost = **23**

d) Then select $J_1 M_4$ and $J_2 M_2$ 4th solution

Minimum cost = **23**

e) Then select $J_1 M_4$ & $J_2 M_3$ further 5th solution

Minimum cost = **23**

Example

A company has 5 jobs to be done. The following matrix shows the return in Rs. Of assigning i^{th} machine to j^{th} job. Assign the five jobs to the five jobs to the five machines so as to maximize the total return.

Machine	Job				
	A	B	C	D	E
1	5	11	10	12	4
2	2	4	6	3	5
3	3	12	5	14	6
4	6	14	4	11	7
5	7	9	8	12	5

This is the maximization problem.

Hence subtracting all the elements from the largest element of matrix i.e. 14, get relative loss matrix as follows:

	A	B	C	D	E
1	6	3	4	2	10
2	12	10	8	11	9
3	11	2	9	0	8
4	8	0	10	3	7
5	7	5	6	2	9

Step (I)   Row subtraction / operation

	A	B	C	D	E

1	7	1	2	0	8
2	4	2	0	3	1
3	11	2	9	0	8
4	8	0	10	3	7
5	5	3	4	0	7

a) Column subtraction

	M1	M2	M3	M4
J1	0	2	2	1
J2	3	0	0	1
J3	0	3	2	3
J4	7	1	1	0

As (3 lines < number of rows / column =4)

Therefore there is not optimum solution

Therefore improvement by using smallest uncovered element 'I'

	M1	M2	M3	M4
J1	0	1	1	0
J2	4	0	0	1
J3	0	2	1	2
J4	8	1	1	0

Therefore select column wise: minimum number of line required to cover all zeroes.

Again solution is not optimum, since number of row = 3 < number of column / rows = XXXXX

Therefore, again **Improvement** by using smallest uncovered element = 1

	M1	M2	M3	M4
J1	0	0	0	0
J2	5	0	0	2
J3	0	1	0	2
J4	8	0	0	0

Therefore 4 lines are required to cover all zeroes = number of rows / column = 4

Therefore => The problem have multiple optimum solutions

(As all rows and columns have more than one single unmarked zeroes)

a) Select J1M1: 1st Solution.

	M1	M2	M3	M4
J1	[0]	0	0	0
J2	5	[0]	0	2
J3	0	1	[0]	2
J4	8	0	0	[0]

	M1	M2	M3	M4
	[0]			

J1	0	0	0	0
J2	5	$\boxed{0}$	0	2
J3	0	1	$\boxed{0}$	2
J4	8	0	0	$\boxed{0}$

Therefore optimum assignment as

$J_1 \rightarrow M_2$, $J_2 \rightarrow M_3$, J3$\rightarrow$ M_3& J4$\rightarrow$ M_4

Therefore minimum cost   =   4+7+9+4+3

=   **23**

C) Then select $J_1 M_3$ 3rd solution

Minimum cost = **23**

d) Then select $J_1 M_4$ and $J_2 M_2$ 4th solution

Minimum cost   =   **23**

e) Then select $J_1 M_4$& $J_2 M_3$ further 5th solution

Minimum cost   =   **23**

Example

A company has 5 jobs to be done. The following matrix shows the return in Rs. Of assigning ith machine to jth job. Assign the five jobs to the five jobs to the five machines so as to maximize the total return.

Machine	Job				
	A	**B**	**C**	**D**	**E**
1	5	11	10	12	4
2	2	4	6	3	5

3	3	12	5	14	6
4	6	14	4	11	7
5	7	9	8	12	5

This is the maximization problem.

Hence subtracting all the elements from the largest element of matrix i.e. 14, get relative loss matrix as follows :

	A	B	C	D	E
1	6	3	4	2	10
2	12	10	8	11	9
3	11	2	9	0	8
4	8	0	10	3	7
5	7	5	6	2	9

Step (i)   Row subtraction / operation

	A	B	C	D	E
1	7	1	2	0	8
2	4	2	0	3	1

3	11	2	9	0	8
4	8	0	10	3	7
5	5	3	4	0	7

Step (ii)   Column subtraction

	A	B	C	D	E
1	3	1	2	0	7
2	0	2	0	3	0
3	7	2	9	0	7
4	4	0	10	3	6
5	1	3	4	0	6

Step (iii)   Draw line / Improvement

	A	B	C	D	E
1	3	1	2	0	7
2	0	2	0	3	0

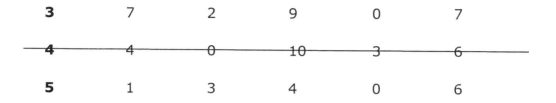

3	7	2	9	0	7
~~4~~	~~4~~	~~0~~	~~10~~	~~3~~	~~6~~
5	1	3	4	0	6

Therefore => Total number of lines = 3 < number of rows/column = 5

Therefore => solution is not optimum

Step (iv)   Iˢᵗ improvement using '1'

	A	B	C	D	E
1	3	1	2	0	7
~~2~~	~~0~~	~~2~~	~~0~~	~~3~~	~~0~~
3	7	2	9	0	7
4	4	0	10	3	6
5	1	3	4	0	6

Therefore Number of line = 4 < number of rows = 5

Therefore solution is not optimum

Therefore 2ⁿᵈ Improvement by using '1'

	A	B	C	D	E

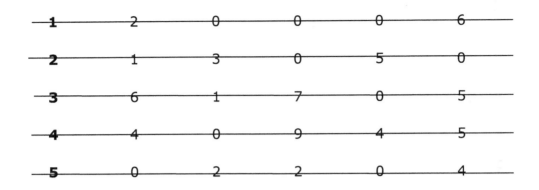

1	2	0	0	0	6
2	1	3	0	5	0
3	6	1	7	0	5
4	4	0	9	4	5
5	0	2	2	0	4

Therefore => number of lines = 5= number of rows/ columns.

Therefore => solution is optimum

Step (v)   Make Assignment

	A	B	C	D	E
1	2	0	[0]	0	6
2	1	3	0	5	[0]
3	6	1	7	0	5
4	4	[0]	9	4	5
5	[0]	2	2	0	4

Hence the optimum assignment are :

(1→ C, 2 → E, 3 → D, 4 → B,   5 → A)

Consider original profit figures, the total profit

=   10+5+14+14+7

=   **50**

Example:

Solve the problem of job assignments to minimize the cost.

Jobs		Employees				
		E1	E2	E3	E4	E5
	J1	10	5	13	15	16
	J2	03	09	18	13	06
	J3	10	07	02	02	02
	J4	07	11	09	07	12
	J5	07	09	10	04	12

→ The given problem is of minimization of the cost

Therefore Hungarian method

Step (I): Row operation / subtraction

	E1	E2	E3	E4	E5
J1	5	0	8	10	11
J2	0	6	15	10	03
J3	08	05	0	0	0
J4	0	4	2	0	5
J5	3	5	6	0	8

Step2:

a) Draw line (Row-wise)

	E1	E2	E3	E4	E5
J1	5	0	8	10	11
J2	0	6	15	10	03
J3	08	05	0	0	0

J4	0	4	2	0	5
J5	3	5	6	0	8

Step (2)   **(b)   Draw line (column wise)**

	E1	E2	E3	E4	E5
J1	5	0	8	10	11
J2	0	6	15	10	03
~~J3~~	~~08~~	~~05~~	~~0~~	~~0~~	~~0~~
J4	0	4	2	0	5
J5	3	5	6	0	8

Therefore Hence the number of line to cover all zero = 4

Therefore **from step (2) – (a) & step (2) – (b)**

Step (2) - (b) required minimum number of **line i.e. '4'** to cover all zeroes.

Use step (2) – (b) for further reduction

Therefore number of line required to cover all zero = 4 < number of rows / column. Therefore => solution is not optimum

Therefore Ist Improvement

Step (3)   Ist Improvement by using element '2"

	E1	E2	E3	E4	E5
J1	5	0	8	10	11
J2	0	6	15	10	03
J3	08	05	0	0	0
J4	0	4	2	0	5
J5	3	5	4	0	8

Therefore number of line required to cover all zeroes = 5 = number of rows / column

Therefore solution is optimum XXX

Make Assignment

Hence the number of lines to cover all zero = 5

And number of rows / column = 5

Therefore => solution is optimum

Therefore make the assignment

See Step (2) – (b)

Step (4)   Make Assignment

	E1	E2	E3	E4	E5
J1	5	0	8	10	11
J2	[0]	[0]	15	10	03
J3	08	05	0	0	[0]
J4	0	4	[0]	0	5
				[0]	

J5	3	5	6	0	8

Therefore optimal assignment policy as

$J_1 \rightarrow E_2$, $J_2 \rightarrow E_1$, $J3 \rightarrow E_5$, $J4 \rightarrow F_3$ & $J5 \rightarrow E_4$

And

Therefore optimal cost with respect to original cost matrix.

$$= \quad 5+3+2+9+4$$

Optimal cost $\quad = \quad$ **23** is required answer

Multiple optimum solution example

Example :

A project work consist of four major jobs for which an equal number of contractors have submitted tenders. The tender amount quoted (in lakh's of rupees) is given in the matrix.

Contractors	Jobs				
	a	**b**	**c**	**d**	**e**
1	10	24	30	15	
2	16	22	28	12	
3	12	20	32	10	
4	9	26	34	16	

Find assignment which minimizes the total cost of the project.

Given problem belongs to minimization type

Therefore **Step (i)**   **Row op^n / Sub^n**

	a	b	C	d
1	0	14	20	5
2	04	10	16	0
3	2	10	22	0
4	0	17	25	7

Step (ii) Collocation operation / Subtraction

	a	b	C	d
1	0	4	4	5
2	4	0	0	0
3	2	0	6	0
4	0	7	9	7

Therefore => Total number of line = 3 < total number of rows or column = 5

Therefore solution is not optimum

Therefore **Ist Improvement using '4' :-**

	a	b	C	d
1	0	0	0	1
2	8	0	0	0
3	6	0	6	0
4	0	3	5	3

Therefore Total number of lines = Number of rows / column = 4

Therefore solution is **optimum**

Step (iii) **Make Assignment** is as follows

	a	b	c	d
1	0	0	0	1
2	8	0	0	0
3	6	0	6	0
4	[0]	3	5	3

Therefore single unmarked zero only at 4a can be marked ( ) and cancelled zero at 1a.

But, All the rows 2,3 & 1 have more than one unmarked zeros

Therefore example belongs to multiple maximum number zeroes

i.e. **3 zeroes**

Therefore select the position 1b   2c & 2d   & find optimum solution.

a) Selecting 2b then making assignment as

	a	b	c	d
1	0	0	[0]	1
2	8	[0]	0	0
3	6	0	6	[0]
4	[0]	3	5	3

⇨ Optimal assignment as

1 -> c, 2 -> b, 3 -> d, 4 -> a

And optimal cost with reference to the

Original matrix

= 30+22+10+9

= **71** .... (a)

b) Selecting 2c then making assignment as

	a	b	c	d
1	0	0	0	1
2	8	0	0	0
3	6	0	6	0
4	0	3	5	3

a) Selecting 2c then making assignment as

	a	b	c	d
1	0	0	0	1
2	8	0	0	0
3	6	0	6	0
4		3	5	3

⇨ Optimal assignment as

⇨ 1-> c, 2 -> c, 3 -> b, 4 -> a

& optimal cost with reference to the original matrix.

$$= \quad 30+12+20+9$$

$$= \quad \mathbf{71} \qquad \text{.................................} \quad (c)$$

Therefore (a), (b) and (c)

All these optimal solution (multiple) give the

Optimum cost as **71**.

(Multiple optimum solution)

Example : Solve the problem of job assignments to minimize the cost.

Technicians		J1	J2	J3	J4	J5	J6
				Jobs			
	T1	2	5	8	2	7	9
	T2	6	7	8	6	2	7
	T3	6	9	4	3	8	5
	T4	5	2	8	4	9	6
	T5	6	3	8	5	2	7

Therefore given problem belongs to minimization of cost from the given information. We need to add fourth row with **Dummy element '1'**

Therefore reduced matrix as follows

	J1	J2	J3	J4	J5	J6

T1	2	5	8	2	7	9
T2	6	7	8	6	2	7
T3	6	9	4	3	8	5
T4	5	2	8	4	9	6
T5	6	3	8	5	2	7
Dummy	0	0	0	0	0	0

Step (1)   **Row optimum / subtraction**

Each column contain lower element zero '0'

Row subtraction is same as column subtraction

	J1	**J2**	**J3**	**J4**	**J5**	**J6**
T1	0	3	6	0	5	7
T2	4	5	6	4	0	5
T3	3	6	1	0	5	2
T4	3	0	6	2	7	4
T5	4	1	6	3	0	5
Dummy	0	0	0	0	0	0

Number of lines required to cover all zeroes -= 5

& number of rows / column = 6

Therefore solution is not optimum

Step (iii)   1st improvement by using '1'

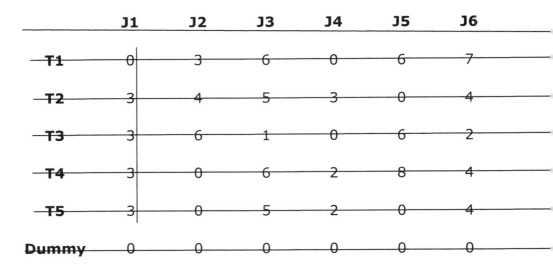

	J1	J2	J3	J4	J5	J6
T1	0	3	6	0	6	7
T2	3	4	5	3	0	4
T3	3	6	1	0	6	2
T4	3	0	6	2	8	4
T5	3	0	5	2	0	4
Dummy	0	0	0	0	0	0

Therefore   number of lines required to cover all zeroes = 6

& number of rows / column = 6

Therefore   both are same

Therefore   solution is **optimum**

Step (iv)   Make assignment

	J1	J2	J3	J4	J5	J6
T1	[0]	3	6	0	6	7
T2	3	4	5	3	[0]	4
T3	3	6	1	[0]	6	2
T4	3	[0]	6	2	8	4
T5	3	0	5	2	0	4
Dummy	0	0	[0]	0	0	[0]

Since, 'Dummy' row contain more than on Unmarked zeroes i.e. '2' zeroes at Position **'Dummy J_3'** and **Dummy J_6**

Therefore prob. belongs multiple optimal solutions.

a) Selecting Dummy J_3 first

Optimal assignment as
$T_1 \rightarrow J_1$, $T_2 \rightarrow J_5$, $T_3 \rightarrow J_4$, $T_4 \rightarrow J_2$
Dummy $= J_3$
& optimal solution I what reference to original table / matrix
$$= \quad 2+2+3+2+0$$
$$= \quad \mathbf{9}$$

b) Selecting Dummy J_6 second

Therefore optimal assignment as

& optimal solution with refer to original matrix

$$= \quad 2+2+3+2+0$$

$$= \quad \mathbf{9} \quad \text{From (a) \& (b) all the optimal solution}$$

Example :

A company has to assign four workers A, B, C & D to four jobs W, X, Y & X the cost matrix is given below

	W	X	Y	Z
A	1000	1200	400	900

B	600	500	300	800
C	200	300	400	500
D	600	700	300	1000

Find optimal assignment for minimization.

Prohibited Assignments:

There are indicated by putting a dash (-) or cross (x) at the prohibited positions. To solve this problem.

i)   For a **minimization** problem assume **(+)cost** for the prohibited position and process further as usual.

ii)   For a **maximization** problem assume **(-) profit** for the prohibited positions and proceed further as usual.

Example (1)

Consider a problem of assiging 4 clerks to 4 task. The time (in hours) required to complete task are given. Clerk 2 can not be assigned to **task A** and **Clerk 3** can not be assigned to **task B**.
Find the optimum assignment schedule**.**

	Task			
	A	**B**	**C**	**D**
1	4	7	8	6
2	--	8	7	4
3	3	--	8	3
4	6	6	4	2

This is the minimization problem

Therefore by default assignment example is of type **minimization** also we required to find required time Therefore this examples is of

The Assignment with **minimization.**

Where the assignments 2 to A and 3 to B are prohibited, Hence assume **(+00)** time for **2 to A & 3 to B** and solve further by using hungarian method.

	A	B	C	D
1	4	7	8	6
2	∞	8	7	4
3	3	∞	8	3
4	6	6	4	2

Step (i)   Row operation

	A	B	C	D
1	0	3	4	2
2	∞	4	3	0
3	0	∞	5	0
4	4	4	2	0

(Note: - ∞-4=∞)

Step (ii)   Column operation

	A	B	C	D
1	0	0	2	2
2	∞	1	1	0
3	0	∞	3	0
4	4	1	0	0

(Note: - $\infty-0=\infty$ $\infty-3=\infty$)

Therefore Total no of lines required to cover all zeroes = 4

= number of lines / Rows

Therefore solution is optimum

Therefore -> makes Assignment.

Step (iii)   Make Assignment

	A	B	C	D
1	0	$\boxed{0}$	2	2
2	∞	1	1	$\boxed{0}$
3	$\boxed{0}$	∞	3	0
4	4	1	$\boxed{0}$	0

Therefore optimal policy as

1→ B, 2 → B, 3 → A, 4 → C

And with reference from original matrix

Total optimum (minimum) time required

$$= \quad 7+4+3+4$$
$$= \quad \textbf{18} \text{ Hours}$$

Example (2)

A airline company has drown up a new flight schedule involving five flights. To assist in allocating five pilots to the flights it has asked them to **stale the preference score** by giving each of flight a **number out of 10. The higher the number**, the **greater is the preference. (Therefore note this problem goes to maximization** certain of these flights are unsuitable to some pilots owing to some domestic reasons. These have been marked with an **X.**

What should be the allocation of the pilots to flights in order to meet **as many preference as possible (=> problem is maximization)**

<table>
<tr><th colspan="7">Flight Number</th></tr>
<tr><th></th><th></th><th>1</th><th>2</th><th>3</th><th>4</th><th>5</th></tr>
<tr><td rowspan="4">Pilot</td><td>A</td><td>8</td><td>2</td><td>X</td><td>5</td><td>4</td></tr>
<tr><td>B</td><td>10</td><td>9</td><td>2</td><td>8</td><td>4</td></tr>
<tr><td>C</td><td>5</td><td>4</td><td>9</td><td>6</td><td>X</td></tr>
<tr><td>D</td><td>3</td><td>6</td><td>2</td><td>8</td><td>7</td></tr>
</table>

	E	5	6	10	4	3

⇨ This is the maximization problem with prohibited assignment

Therefore late assume element (-00) for the unsuitable

Position A_3 and C_5

Therefore reduced matrix become

		Flight Number				
		1	2	3	4	5
Pilot	A	8	2	$-\infty$	5	4
	B	10	9	2	8	4
	C	5	4	9	6	$-\infty$
	D	3	6	2	8	7
	E	5	6	10	4	3

Let us obtain the relative loss matrix by subtracting all its elements from the largest element i.e.10

Therefore reduced matrix become.

Flight Number							
		1	**2**	**3**	**4**	**5**	
Pilot	**A**	2	8	<u>5</u>	6	4	
	B	0	1	8	2	6	
	C	5	6	1	4	<u>-∞</u>	
	D	7	4	8	2	3	
	E	5	4	0	6	7	

(Note:- 10-(-∞)=10+∞=∞)

Step (i)   Row operation

	1	2	3	4	5
A	0	6	∞	3	4
B	0	1	8	2	6

C	4	5	0	3	∞
D	5	2	6	0	1
E	5	4	0	6	7

Step (ii)   Column operation

	1	**2**	**3**	**4**	**5**
A	0	5	∞	3	3
B	0	0	8	2	5
C	4	4	0	3	∞
D	5	1	6	0	0
E	5	3	0	6	6

(Note:- $\infty - 0 = \infty$ $\infty - 1 = \infty$)

Step (iii)   Draw line

Here maximization number of zero row wise = 2

Maximization number of zero column wise = 2

Therefore   => tie

(a)   If we select row, 1st to draw line then, total number of line required to cover all zero = 4

	1	**2**	**3**	**4**	**5**
~~**A**~~	0	5	∞	3	3
~~**B**~~	0	0	8	2	5
C	4	4	0	3	∞
~~**D**~~	5	1	6	0	0
E	5	3	0	6	6

(a)   If we select column, first to draw line then

Total number of line required to cover all zero = 4

	1	2	3	4	5
A	0	5	∞	3	3
B	0	0	8	2	5
C	4	4	0	3	∞
D	5	1	6	0	0
E	5	3	0	6	6

Therefore (a) & (b) => same number of lines to cover all

Zeros = use any one

Say use **step (iii)** → **a** for further calculation

Therefore => Total number of line required to cover all

Zero = 4 < number of rows / column = 5

Therefore => solution is not optimum

Therefore => Make improvement by using

Smallest uncovered element of matrix

Step (iii) - XXXX i.e. using '3'

Step (iv)   1ˢᵗ Improvement using '3'

	1	2	3	4	5
A	0	5	∞	3	3
B	0	0	11	2	5
C	1	1	0	0	∞
D	5	1	9	0	0
E	2	0	0	3	3

(Note: - ∞+3=∞ ∞-3=∞)

Therefore Total number of lines required to cover

    All zeroes = 5 = number of rows / column

Hence solution optimum

Therefore => Make Assignment As

	1	2	3	4	5
A	$\boxed{0}$	5	∞	3	3
B	0	$\boxed{0}$	11	2	5
C	1	1	0	$\boxed{0}$	∞
D	5	1	9	0	$\boxed{0}$
E	2	0	$\boxed{0}$	3	3

Therefore optimal Assignment policy as

      A→ 1, B → 2, C→ 4, D → 5, e → 3

        =   8+9+6+7+10

        =   **40** is the required answer.

Mathematical Representation of Assignment Problem

    To examine the nature of an assignment problem, suppose there are 'n' jobs to be performed and 'n' persona are available to do this job.

    Assume that each person can do each job at a time.

    Let Cij to be the cost (payment) if i^{th} person is assignment to j^{th} job.

    The problem is to find an assignment (i.e. which job should be assign to which person), so that total cost for **performing** all jobs is minimum.

The problem of this kind is **called assignment problem / method.**

The assignment model can be stated as nxn matrix (Cij), which is called cost matrix where entry Cij denote the cwt, when i^{th} person is assigned to j^{th} job.

Mathematical Representation

Persons		Jobs						a_i
		J1	J2	J3	J4	---------------	J_n	1
	1	C_{11}	C_{12}	C_{13}	C_1	--------------- ----	C_{1n}	1
	2	C_{21}	C_{22}	C_{23}	C_{24}	--------------- ----	C_{2n}	1
	3	C_{31}	C_{32}	C_{33}	C_{34}	--------------- -----		
	... .	....	....	....	....	....	....	....
	... ...	....	....	....	....	....	....	....

	n	C_{n1}	C_{n2}	C_{n3}	C_{n4}		C_{n1}	1
	b_j	1	1	1	1	....	1	

Suppose

Xij represents an assignment when i^{th}

  person is assigned to perform j^{th} job.

Hence   Xij   = 0 if i^{th} person is not assigned j^{th} job

              = 1 if j^{th} person is assigned j^{th} job

Thus, objective function is to minimize the

  Total cost is

Subject to the constraints

i.e. **and**

Express / Explain the following problem as LPP

Contractors	Projects			
	A	**B**	**C**	**D**
I	7	5	9	10
II	3	7	5	8
III	7	4	8	9
IV	8	7	5	2

Therefore By default assignment problem is of type Minimization

Therefore above is problem is of type **minimization** Therefore **objective function**, by definition of problem formula (XXX ofan assignment method is

a) Subject to the constrains on **contractors (Row wise)**i.e.

b) Subject of the constrains on projects **(Column wise)**i.e.and

c) **Explain / Express the following assignment problem as LPP**

	A	B	C	D	E
I	6	4	9	2	9
II	9	3	7	1	2
III	4	1	4	5	6
IV	2	8	1	3	3
V	6	7	9	7	2

→ In the above Assignment problem not mention whether it is minimization/ maximization

Therefore by default assignment problem is of type **minimization.**

Therefore the definition problem formulation of assignment method

a) Subject to the **constraint on numbers** (I, II, III, IV, xxxx)

b) Subject to the **constrain** is on **Alphabets** (i.e. A,B,C,D & E)

c) **Explain / Express the following assignment problem as LPP**

	A	B	C	D	E
I	3	8	5	3	8
II	2	4	4	6	8
III	3	3	5	7	4
IV	5	4	2	2	7
V	8	1	8	5	3

d)

Chapter II

TRANSPORTATION PROBLEMS

It is a typical operation and Research technique intended to establish a least cost route for the transportation of goods from the **sources** (say a company's production plants) to the various **destinations** (say its warehouse)

Terminology of Transportation Problem:

1. **Balanced Transportation Problem :**

   Here total capacity of supply points or sources is equal to the total demand at the destinations.

2. **Unbalanced Transportation Problem :**

   Here total supply is not equal to the total demand.

3. Transportation Table :

It is used to represents the data about supply at sources, demand at destinations and per unit transportation cost from each sources to each destination.

Example

Plant	Warehouse			
	Delhi	Pune	Bangalore	Supply
Mumbai	10 (300)	3 (300)	6	1000
Chennai	15 (200)	10	4 (1000)	1200
Kolkata	11 (200)	15	12 (600)	800
Demand	700	700	1600	3000

4. Dummy sources of destination :

This is represented by **adding** an **extra row** or **column** to the transportation table with **'0' per unit cost** for each of its cells.

5. **Initial Feasible solutions :**

It is a solution that satisfies the **supply** and **demand** conditions and yet it may or may not be **optimum solution.**

There are three methods to obtain optimum solution
- North West Corner Method (NWCM)

- Least Cost Method (LCM) and

- Vogel's Approximation Method (VAM)

6. **Optimum Solution :**

It is the feasible solution which also gives the transportation plan with minimum total cost.

This obtained by using
- Stepping Stone Method or

- Modified Distribution Method (MODI Method)

General Procedure for solving a Transportation Problem

Step 1: Define the objective function to be minimized with the constraints imposed on the problem.

Step 2 : Set up the transportation table with 'm' rows **(sources)** and 'n' columns **(Destinations)**, along with their supply and demand figures as well as the per unit cost figure.

Step 3: Add dummy rows or column, if necessary.

Step 4: Develop the initial feasible solution by using method either NWCM, LCM or VAM.

Step 5: Examine the **feasibility** of the initial solution

> Note
>
> The solution is feasible if it has allocations at (m+n-1) number of cells at independent positions.
>
> That is it has (m+n-1) in depended occupied cells.

Step 6: Test the solution, if found feasible for optimality by finding out the opportunity costs for all unoccupied or empty cells.

Non-negative (i.e. zero / positive) opportunity cost for all empty cells indicates that the solution is optimal.

Step 7: If the solution is not optimal, we improve it by using the Stepping Stone Method / MODI Method.

Step 8: **Repeat** the **step 5,6, and 7**until an optimal solution is obtained.

Methods for findings Initial feasible solution

I) North West Corner Method (NWCM) :

Step 1: Select the North-West corner cell in the transportation table, and allocate **as many units** as possible to it, after checking the **supply** (in the row) and the **demand** (in the column) position for the cell.

Step 2: Reduce the **supply** and **demand** figure for the corresponding **row** and **column** accordingly.

Step 3: Cover the row or column (i.e. draw line where the supply or demand figure gets fully exhausted **(i.e. it becomes '0')**

Step 4: Go to step (i) and repeat the procedure until total supply is **fully allocated to the cells** so as to fulfill the total demand.

Note

Though it is easy, it requires many further improvements to the optimum solution.

Example I

1. Consider the following to transportation table with supply, demand and per unit cost figure. This is **balanced table** with **total demand = total supply = 125**

	D_1	D_2	D_3	Supply
S_1	3	2	1	20

		2	4	1	50
S$_2$					
S$_3$		3	5	2	30
S$_4$		4	6	7	25
Demand	40		30	55	125

Solution:

Step 1 :

    i)   Choose the North-West corner i.e. **S$_1$D$_1$**

        The row wise supply is 20 and

        Column wise demand is 40 for this cell

        Hence we can assign at **most 20 units** to it.

    ii)   After assigning 20 units,

        The supply becomes (20-20) = 0

        And the demand D$_1$ reduces to 40-20=20

   iii)   This, cover row S1, Now its **supply** has been fully used **reduced Matrix become**

	D$_1$	D$_2$	D$_3$	Supply
S$_1$	20 3	2	1	20 , 0
S$_2$	2	4	1	50

S_3	3	5	2	30
S_4	4	6	7	25
Demand	40 , 20	30	55	125

Step 2 :

Repeat the Step 1, i.e. select North West Corner cell i.e. S_2D_1

- We can assign at most **20 units** to it

- After Assigning 20 units

Column demand get reduces to '0' i.e. D_1
& row supply get reduces to 50-20=30
  i.e. S_2

Therefore reduced matrix becomes

	D_1	D_2	D_3	Supply
S_1	3 (20)	2	1	20 , 0
S_2	2 (20)	4	1	50 , 30
S_3	3	5	2	30

S₄	4	6	7	25
Demand	4̶0̶ , 2̶0̶, 0	30	55	125

Cover 'D₁" as its demand fully utilized.

Step 3.   :

Make the allocation at **S₂D₂** (North West Corner Cell)
of **30 units**

Raw supply reduces to **zero** and column
demand also become **zero**

	D₁	D₂	D₃	Supply
S₁	3 ⃝20	2	1	2̶0̶ , 0
S₂	2 ⃝20	4 ⃝30	1	5̶0̶ , 3̶0̶ , 0
S₃	3	5	2	30
S₄	4	6	7	25

Demand	4Ø , 2Ø, 0	30 , 0	55	125

Step 4. :

Now only onecolumn i.e. D_3 is remain with S_3D_3 and S_4D_3

Therefore,

Make the allocation directly to them of the remaining **30 units** and **25 units** supply. This automatically satisfies the demand of for **55 units**.

	D₁	D₂	D₃	Supply
S₁	3 \ 20	2	1	2̶0̶ , 0
S₂	2 \ 20	4 \ 30	1	5̶0̶ ,3̶0̶ , 0
S₃	3	5	2 \ 30	3̶0̶ ,0

S_4	4	6	7	25,0
			25	
Demand	40 , 20, 0	30 , 0	55 , 0	125

Thus here we are getting a plan to transport

20 units from S_1 to D_1
20 units from S_2 to D_1
30 units from S_2 to D_2
30 units from S_3 to D_3
25 units from S_4 to D_3

Therefore **Total cost** = 20(3) +20(2) + 30(4) + 30(2) + 25(7)

= **455**

Note

...ver, number of occupied cells = 5 (i.e.S1D1, S2D1 etc)

Which are less than (m+n-1 = 4+3-1 = 6)

Therefore the solution is **not feasible**.

II.Least Cost Method (LCM) or Matrix Minimum Method

Here we are going to make allocation to the minimum cost cell in the table.

Step 1.

i)   Select a cell with minimum unit transportation cost form the table.

ii)   If there are **more than one cells** with **minimum** unit transportation cost, then select that cell among them where more number of units can be allocated

(after considering their row supply and column demand.)

iii)   If there is a **tie** again, then **select** as **cell randomly** from them.

Step 2.   Allocate maximum possible number of units to it reduces the corresponding **Row Supply** &**condition demand**.

Step 3.   Repeat the step (1)and step (2) until entire supply is exhausted to fulfill entire demand.

Example II

We consider the same problem as in example I.
And use **LCM Method** to solve

	D_1	D_2	D_3	Supply
S_1	3	2	1	20
S_2	2	4	1 50	50 , 0
S_3	3	5	2	30

S$_4$	4	6	7	25
Demand	40	30	55 , 0	125

Step I.   In the above select a least cost cell.

There are two such cells i.e. S3D3 and S2D3 both having unit cost 1

Therefore =>**Tie**

Therefore from problem by observing Row Supply and Column Demand

We can allocate   **20** units at S$_1$D$_3$ and

50 units at S$_2$D$_3$

Therefore select S$_2$D$_3$ and allocate 50 units to it

So as to row supply reduces it becomes **zero**

And column demand get minimized to **5**

⇨ Cover **row S$_2$**

Step II.   For Reduced table Repeat procedure (I) / **Step 1.**

Select S$_1$D$_3$ and allocate **5 units.**

Therefore =>**cover column D$_3$**

	D$_1$	**D$_2$**		**D$_3$**	**Supply**
S$_1$	3	2	5	1	20 , 15,
S$_2$	2	4	50	1	50 , 0

S₃	3	5	2	30
S₄	4	6	7	25
Demand	40	30	55̶, 5̶, 0	

Step III. Make allocation at S_1D_2 of 15 units

	D₁	D₂	D₃	Supply
S₁	3	2 ⟨15⟩	1 ⟨5⟩	2̶0̶, 1̶5̶, 0
S₂	2	4	1 ⟨50⟩	5̶0̶, 0
S₃	3	5	2	30
S₄	4	6	7	25
Demand	40	3̶0̶, 15	5̶5̶, 5̶, 0	

Step IV. Make the allocation at S_3D_1 of 30 units

	D₁	D₂	D₃	Supply
S₁	3	2	1	20
S₂	2	4	1 ⟨50⟩	5̶0̶, 0

S₃	3 $\quad$ (30)	5	2	30
S₄	4	6	7	25
Demand	40	30 , 0	55 , 0	

Step V. For the remaining row S_4 with Position S_4D_2 make the Allocation directly gets

	D_1	D_2	D_3	**Supply**
S₁	3	2	1	20
S₂	2	4	1 $\quad$ (50)	50 , 0
S₃	3	5	2	30

S$_4$	4	6	7	25
Demand	40	30 , 0	55 , 0	

Therefore total cost   = 15(2) + 5(1) + 50(1) + 30(3)

$$= 10(4) + 15(6)$$

$$= \mathbf{305}$$

Also, since there are **m+n-1 = 4+3-1 = 6**

Number of independent cells, therefore the solution is **Feasible.**

III   **Vogel's Approximation Method (VAM)**

Here we go on **making allocations** to the **minimum cost cells** of a **row** or **column** for which **penalty** for **not making an allocation is high**.

Step I   Compute the penalty (i.e. the difference between two smallest unit cost figures for the cells) for each row and columns.

Step II   Identify the **row** or **column** with **highestpenalty** and **choose** the **cell** with **smallest per unit cost in it.**

Note

If there is tie for highest penalties, select the row or column, containing minimum cost cell among them.

If there is tie **again**, then select that cell where **maximization** allocation is possible or we can select it **randomly.**

Step III Allocate the maximization possible units to the selected cell and reduce its row supply and column demand accordingly.

Step IV **Re-compute the penalties for the deduced table** (If a row (column) has been covered the row (column) **penalties** remain unchanged.)

Repeat the above procedure until the entire demand and supply fully gets exhausted.

Example

We consider the same problem as in
Example **1**: and Example **2**

Step I **Compute the penalty**

	D_1	D_2	D_3	Supply	Penalty
S_1	3	2	1	20	2-1=1
S_2	2	4	1	50	2-1=1
S_3	3	5	2	30	3-2=1
S_4	4	6	7	25	6-4=2
Demand	40	30	55		

Penalty	3-2=1	4-2=2	1-1=0		

Step II   Identify the row/ column containing highest penalty

Therefore   Row S_4 & column D_2 have highest

Penalty = 2 Therefore => there is tie

Therefore   Select the one containing minimum cost cell

S_4D_1 cell cost = 4

& S_1D_2 cell cost = 2

Therefore select **S_1D_2** and make the allocation
of **20 units** to it.

	D_1	D_2		D_3	Supply	Penalty
S_1	3	(20)	2	1	2̶0̶ ,0	1
S_2	2		4	1	50	1
S_3	3		5	2	30	1
S_4	4		6	7	25	2
Demand	40	3̶0̶,	10	55		
Penalty	1	2		0		

Therefore,   we cover S_1 as its supply gets fully exhausted

Reduced taste as above.

Step III. **Re-compute** the **penalties**, As a row has been covered, the row penalties will remain unchanged, while only the column penalties will change as shown below

	D_1	D_2		D_3	Supply	Penalty
S_1	3	(20)	2	1	2̸0 0	1
S_2	2		4	1	50	1
S_3	3		5	2	30	1
S_4	4		6	7	25	2
Demand	40	3̸0,	10	55		
Penalty	1	1		1		

Row S4 has highest penalties. Hence select it and make maximum allocation to it.

Cell S4D1 have smallest per unit cost = 4

Select S4D1 and make allocation to it

	D_1		D_2		D_3	Supply	Penalty
S_1		3	(20)	2	1	2̸0 0	1
S_2		2		4	1	50	2-1 = 1
S_3		3		5	2	30	3-2 = 1
S_4	(25)	4		6	7	25, 0	2
Demand	4̸0. 15		3̸0,	10	55		
Penalty	3-2=1		5-4=1		2-1=1		

And also recomputed the penalties

Therefore the reduced matrix as above

Also cover &**row S_4**

Step IV

All the rows and columns have same penalties

Therefore we select cell S_2D_3 with minimum unit **cost**

And make allocation of **50 units** to it

Therefore =>**row S2 will cover.**

Therefore reduced matrix becomes =>

	D$_1$		D$_2$		D$_3$	Supply	Penalty
S$_1$		3	(20)	2	1	2̶0̶ 0	1
S$_2$		2		4	1	5̶0̶,0	1
S$_3$		3		5	2	30	1
S̶₄̶	(25)	4		6	7	2̶5̶, 0	2
Demand	4̶0̶. 15		3̶0̶, 10		5̶5̶,5		
Penalty	1		1		1		

Step V.

We then make allocation to the remaining cost **row S$_3$** **directly**, to get initial feasible solution as follow.

	D$_1$		D$_2$		D$_3$		Supply	Penalty
S$_1$		3	(20)	2		1	2̶0̶ 0	1
S$_2$					(20)	1	5̶0̶,0	1
S$_3$	(15)	3		5	(5)	2	30,2̶5̶,10,0	1
S$_4$	(25)	4		6		7	2̶5̶, 0	2

Demand	40, 15	30, / 10,0	55,5,0		
Penalty	1	1	1		

⇨ Here the total cost = 20(2) + 50(1) + 15(3)

+ 10(5) + 5(2) +25 (4)

= **295**

Also number of occupied cells = m+n-1 = 4+3-1= 6

Therefore solution is feasible

:

⇨ Solution obtained from **EX-1, EX-2, EX-3**

Indicates by using VAM gives the minimum cost

Among all these three methods.

⇨ This is the best method to get initial

Feasible solution **which need very few** **IMPROVEMENT**

Further to **get the optimum solution.**

Find the initial solution for the following problem (i) NVCM, (ii) VAM the supply and demand figure are given.

	W$_1$	W$_2$	W$_3$	W$_4$	S

P_1	190	300	500	100	70
P_2	700	300	400	600	90
P_3	400	100	400	200	180
D	50	80	70	140	340

Method for finding the optimum solution

Once the initial solution is obtained, we **verifyitforfeasibility** by **findingthe** number of occupied cells.

If the number of occupied cells is **equalto the m+n-1** then the **solution** is **feasible, otherwise it is called as a case of degeneracy.**

If the solution is feasible we improve it further by using steeping stone method / MODI Method to obtain the optimum solution.

A] Modified Distribution Method (MODI Method) or UV Method

Step 1: Determine the initial feasible solution and write that it is feasible.

That is it has (m+n-1) independent occupied cells.

Step 2: Determine the row numbers (ded as ui i.e. u1, u2, ... etc.) and column numbers (ded at Uj i.e. U1, U2 ...... etc.) by using the formula.

XXXXXXXXXX   for each **occupied** cells.

- Cij is the per unit transportation cost.

- **Choose here one of the various of U1 or Uj is 0**

  Arbitrarily (Prefer that row / column having Maximum number of occupied cell)

- Then use formula for finding remaining values.

Step 3: Consider the **unoccupied** cells and find **opportunity cost,** by using the formula.

Opportunity cost XXXXXXXXXXXXXXXXXXXXX

Step 4: Check the **sign of all opportunity cost** is all of them are non-negative (i.e. zero or **positive**) then it **implies the solution is optimum.**

Otherwise, it implies that solution is **notobtain** and there is a scope for **furtherimprovement** i.e. **go for step 5.**

Step 5: Select the unoccupied cell **with highest negative opportunity cost.**

(If there is **tie**, then select a cell where more units can be allocated.)

Step 6: For this cell, trace a closed path using most direct path/ route through **at least 3 occupied** and then **back to** the original / **starting unoccupied cells.**

Use only **vertical** and **horizontal lines** and **take turn only at the occupied cells.**

Step 7: **Assign positive** and **negative signs alternately to each corner cells** along the closed path, **starting with positive sign** for the **selecting unoccupied cell.**

Step 8: Find the maximum number of units to be shifted to this unoccupied cell. (These **number are equal** to the **least minimum** of the number of units in the **cells with negative signs**)

Add this **number of units** to the cells with **positive sign** and **subtract** it from the cell with **negative sign** along the closed path.

Step 9: Go to **step 1** and repeat the procedure until an optimum solution is obtained.

Example I

1) Solve the following transportation problem to find its optimum solution.

	W_1	W_2	W_3	W_4	Supply
P_1	190	300	500	100	70
P_2	700	300	400	600	90
P_3	400	100	400	200	180
Demand	50	80	70	140	340

Step 1. Using the least cost Method we get initial **feasible** solution of this balanced transportation problem.

	W_1	W_2	W_3	W_4	Supply
P_1	190	300	500	(70) 100	70
P_2	(20) 700	300	(70) 400	600	90
P_3	(50) 400	(80) 100	400	(70) 200	180
Demand	50	80	70	140	340

Therefore => It has total number of allocation = m+n-1

= 3+4-1

= 6

Hence, the **solution is feasible**

: and total cost = 20(700) +70(100) + 70(400)

= 80(100)+30(400)+70(200)

= **83,000**

Step 2. Assign and determine the row number and column number XXXX

	W_1	W_2	W_3	W_4	Supply	Row No.
P_1	190	300	500	(70) 100	70	$4_1 = -\underline{100}$

P$_2$	(20) 700	300	(70) 400	600	90	4$_2$=<u>300</u>
P$_3$	(30) 400	(80) 00	400	(70) 200	180	4$_3$-=<u>0</u>
D	50	80	70	140		
Column No.	v$_1$=400	v$_2$= 100	v$_3$=100	v$_4$=200		

Choose   XX=0 (Therefore maximum number of allocation at this row)

Therefore by using formula

XXXXXXXXXXXXXXX   find   other   values   for   **occupied cells.**

Therefore

⇨ We get all the **row numbers** and **column numbers.**

Step 3:   To find   the   **opportunity   cost**   XXXXX   for   each **unoccupied cell**

By using formula

Therefore **each unoccupied cell find its opportunity cost**

Step 4:   Since all the unoccupied cell, opportunity cost **are not positive.**

Therefore Solution is Not optimum

Therefore there is further scope for improvement

Step 5:   Select the cell, with **highest negative opportunity cost.**

Therefore cell P_1W_1 have highest **-110** opp. Cost

Step 6 &7 :Trace a direct closed path for this cell using Vertical and Horizontal line, and **taking turn only at the occupied** cells.

We then assign positive and negative sign alternately to the corner, starting with positive sign.

Therefore reduced matrix becomes

	W_1	W_2	W_3	W_4	Supply
P_1	(+) ↑190	300	600	70 (−)100	70
P_2	20 700	300	70 400	600	90
P_3	30 400 (−)	80 100	400	70 200 (+)	180
Demand	50	80	70	140	

Step 8: Find the maximum number of units to be shifted to **cell P_1W_1**

Therefore along the closed path negative sign allocated

To cells P_1W_4 and P_3W_1

And P_1W_4 having **70 units**

P_3W_1 having **30 units**

Therefore => least number between them is**30 units**

Hence we shift 30 units to P_1W_1 along the path

Therefore => For this we add 30 units to positive sign

And we subtract 30 units to negative sign

Therefore, To get an **improved solution as – (Ist Improvement)**

	W$_1$	W$_2$	W$_3$	W$_4$	Supply	
P$_1$	(30) 190	300	500	(40) 100	70	4$_1$
P$_2$	(20) 700	300	(70) 400	600	90	4$_2$
P$_3$	(30) 100	(80) 100	400	(10) 200	180	4$_3$
Demand	50	80	70	140		
	V$_1$	V$_2$	V$_3$	V$_4$		

$$
\begin{aligned}
\text{Total cost} \ &= \ 30(190) + 40(100) + 20(700) \\
&= \ +70(400) + 80(100) + 100(200) \\
&= \ \mathbf{79,700}
\end{aligned}
$$

Step 9: Now (number of step (1) check whether it is Feasible or not

Therefore number of allocation $= 6 = m+n-1 = 3+4-1$

$= 6$

(i) Therefore $=>$**solution is feasible**

$\Rightarrow$ Solution is feasible and check whether it is optimum Yes / Not and improve it **is the required step.**

(ii) **Assign** and **determine** the **row number and column** (XXXXX)

	W₁	W₂	W₃	W₄	Supply	4i Row No.
P₁	(30) 190	300	500	(40) 100	70	$4_1 = 0$
P₂	(20) 700	300	(70) 00	600	90	$4_2 = 510$
P₃	400	(80) 00	400	(10) 200	180	$4_3 = 100$
Demand	50	80	70	140		
Vi col.No.	$v_1 = \underline{190}$	$v_2 = \underline{0}$	$v_3 = \underline{-110}$	$v_4 = \underline{100}$		

Choose

By using formula,

⇨ We get all the row numbers and column number (i.e. XXXXXX)

(iii) **Find the opportunity** cost XXX **for eachunoccupiedcell(** : We write this opportunity cost at lower left hand corner and each unoccupied cell.

By using formula:

Reduced table becomes

	W₁	W₂	W₃	W₄	Supply	4i Row No.
P₁	(30) 190	300 / 300	500 / 610	(40) 100	70	$4_1 = 0$
P₂	(20) 700	300 / -210	(70) 400	600 / -10	90	$4_2 = 510$

P₃	400	100	400	200	180	$4_3=100$
	110	80	410	10		
Demand	50	80	70	140		
col.No.	$v_1=190$	$v_2=0$	$v_3=-110$	$v_4=100$		

(iv) Since all unoccupied cell, opportunity cost

Are **not positive**

Therefore **solution is Not optimum.**

⇨ There is further scope for improvement.

(v) Select the cell, with **highest negative opportunity cost**.

⇨ Cell **P₂W₂** have highest **-210** opportunity cost.

(vi)& (vii) Trace a **direct closed path for this cell**
(turn only at occupied cell)
Then assign Positive and negative sign alternately
To the corner, starting with **Positive sign.**

Reduced Matrix becomes

	W₁	W₂	W₃	W₄	Supply
P₁	30 / 190 (+)	300	500	100 / 40 (−)	70
P₂	20 / 700 (−)	300	400 / 70	600	90
P₃	400	100 / 80 (−)	400	200 / 100 (+)	180

Demand	50	80	70	140	

(vii)   Find the maximum number of units to be shifted to cell **P₂W₂**

Therefore along closed path negative sign allocated to

Cell P2W1, P1W4 and P3W3

P_2W_4 having **20 units**

P_1W_4 having **40 units**

P_3W_1 having **30 units**

Therefore => least number between them is **20 units**

Hence we shift 20 units to P2W2, alone the path.

For this we add 20 units to positive sign

And subtract 20 units to negative sign

Therefore to get an improvement solution as

(IIⁿᵈ improvement)

	W_1	W_2	W_3	W_4	Supply
P_1	50 190	300	500	20 100	70
P_2	700	20 300	70 400	600	90
P_3	400	60 100	400	120 200	180
Demand	50	80	70	140	

Total cost = 50(190) + 20(100) + 20(300) + 60(100) + 120(200)

= **75,500**

This table also has an m=n-1 = 6 occupied cells.

Therefore =>It is feasible solution

Now, **check whether it is optimum Yes/Not**

We, now find XX and XX values and then

Find **XXX and check the solution is optimum or Not**

We directly, write down in table as follows:

	W_1	W_2	W_3	W_4	Supply	4i Row No.
P_1	190 ⟨50⟩	300 □300	500 □400	100 ⟨20⟩	70	$4_1 = 0$
P_2	700 □210	300 □20	400 ⟨70⟩	600 □200	90	$4_2 = 300 - 0 = \underline{300}$
P_3	400 □110	100 ⟨60⟩	400 □200	200 ⟨12⟩	180	$4_3 = 200 - 100 \ 100 =$
Demand	50	80	70	140		
col.No.	$v_1 = 130 - 0 = 190$	$v_2 = 100 - 100 = 0$	$v_3 = 400 - 300 = 100$	$v_4 = 100 - 0 = 100$		

Therefore, Since opportunity cost (Numbers in small square) are **Positive**

Therefore => the solution is optimum

Thus the optimum transportation plan as

Source	Destination	Number of units to be transported	Total cost
P_1	W_1	50	50x190=9500
P_1	W_1	20	20x100=2000
P_2	W_2	20	20x300=6000
P_2	W_2	70	70x400=28000
P_3	W_3	60	60x100=6000
P3	W_3	120	1200x200=24000
			Total Rs.=75,500

Therefore I)   The total cost goes on reducing from

Rs.53,000/-→ Rs.79,700/-→**Rs.75,500/-**

As we make improvement.

2 :

Solve the following transportation problem to find **optimum** solution by using **MODI Method.**

	W_1	W_2	W_3	W_4	Supply
P_1	5	3	6	4	30
P_2	3	4	7	8	15
P_3	5	6	5	8	15
Demand	10	25	18	7	

:

Initial feasible solution obtained by (i.e.total cost) by **VAM** are most probable (i.e. 99%) is equal / **same** to the solution obtained by (i.e. total cost) by **MODI Method**

     Special cases in Transportation Problems.

A]   **Unbalanced Problems:**

-     If the total supply from all the sources is **not equal** to the demand at all destinations, it is an unbalanced transportation problem.

-     It is balanced by introducing dummy row / column as

-     If **total demand** is **greater** than total **supply** and **dummy row** with its **supply is equal** to the

difference between **total demand** and **total supply** (with all its cell as zero)

- If total **supply** is **greater** than total **demand**, add **dummy column** with its demand is equal to the difference between **total supply and total demand** (with all its cell cost as zero)

- Solve the further problem as an usual transportation problem

B]   Multiple optimum solutions:

- This is indicated by **Zero opportunity cost (XXX)** for one or more **unoccupied cells** in the transportation table.

- **Alternate solution** can be **obtained** by **shifting** some **units to this cell** as we **do it** for the cell with a highest **negative** opp. cost in MODI Method.

- This gives us **different transportation plan** with **same** (Minimum) total transportation cost.

Example I

Four petrol deals A,B,C and D require 50, 40, 60 and 40 kl of petrol respectively.   It is possible to supply this from three locations X, Y and Z which have 80, 100 and 50 kl respectively.

The cost in rupees for shipping each kl is shown below

Location	**Dealers**			
	A	B	C	D
X	7	6	6	6
Y	5	7	6	7
Z	8	5	8	6

Determine the most economical supply pattern for the company. Identify an alternate plan. If any.

→ Requirement of petrol / demand

$$= 50+40+60+40 = \textbf{190kl}$$

And supply = 80+100+50 = **230 kl**
Therefore → total supply > total demand
Therefore →It is an unbalance type problem
Therefore →We required to add dummy column (E)
With demand 230 – 190 = **40 kl**
Therefore → problem become balance transportation problem
Reduced Matrix become.

Location	Dealers					Supply
	A	B	C	D	E (Dummy)	
X	7	6	6	6	0	80
Y	5	7	6	7	0	100
Z	8	5	8	6	0	50
Demand	50	40	60	40	40	

Step i) By using VAM check the solution feasible or Not and find total cost. ⓘ II ⓘ II   ⓘ I

	A C	B	D	E	Supply	Penalty
X	7 6	6 ⑩	6 ⑩ 0 ㉚		80,40,10	6←0.0.0 .0← 6
Y	⑳ 6 6	7 ㊿	7	0	100,50,0	5,1,1,1,1⁵
Z	8 ㊵	5	6 ⑩ 0	0	50,10,0	5,1,1³

						2,4
Demand	50,0 40,0 / 60I,10,0		/ 40I,30,0 / 40,0		280	
Penalty	2 ↑ 2	0.0		0.		

Therefore ➔ total number of allocation = **7**

And m+n-1 = 3+5-1 =**7**

Step i) Therefore ➔ Solution is feasible

And non-degeneracy.

And

Total cost   =   10(6)+30(6)+40(0)+50(5)+(6)+40(5)+10(6)

=   **1050**

To obtain the optimum solution by using MODI Method.

Step ii)   Assign and Determine Row number and Column number

	A	B	C	D	E dummy	Supply	Row No $4i$
X	7	6	6	6	0	80	$4_1 = 0$
Y	5	7	6	30	0	100	$4_2 = 0$
Z	8	5	10	50	0	50	$4_3 = 0$

Demand	50	40	60	40	40	230	
Col.No. (vj)	$v_1 = 5$	$v_2 = 5$	$v_3 = 6$	$v_4 = 6$	$v_5 = 0$		

To find XXXXXX for all **occupied** cell using formula

ocupiedcal	$e_{ij} = u_i + v_j$	ai§ vi value
for XC	$6 = 0 + V_3$	$V_3 = 6$
for XD	$6 = 0 + V_4$	$V_4 = 6$
for XE	$0 = 0 + V_5$	$V_5 = 0$
for YA	$5 = 0 + U_{2} + V_1$	$V_1 = 5$
	$\therefore 7 = 5 = 0 + V_1 \therefore \longrightarrow V_1 = 5$	
for YC	$6 = u_2 + V_3 \quad \therefore 6 = u_2 + 6$	$u_2 = 0$
	$\therefore u_2 = 0$	$u_2 = 0$
for zb	$5 = u_3 + v_2$	
	$5 = 0 + v_2 \therefore \longrightarrow V_2 = 5$	$V_2 = 5$
for zo	$6 = u_3 + v_4$	
	$6 = u_3 + 6$	
	$\therefore \longrightarrow u_3 = 0$	$u_3 = 0$

Step iii)   Find opportunity cost i.e. XXXX for all **unoccupied cell**

unoccupied cal.	opp. cost formula $\Delta_{ij} = (ij - (u_i + v_j)$	opp. cost
For XA	$\Delta = 7 - (0+5) = 2$	2
For XB	$\Delta = 6 - (0+5) = 1$	1
For YB	$\Delta = 7 - (0+5) = 2$	2
For YB	$\Delta = 7 - (0+6) = 1$	1
For YE	$\Delta = 0 - (0+0) = 0$	0 *

For ZA	Δ = 8-(0+5) =3	3
For ZC	Δ = 8-(0+6) =2	2
For ZE	Δ = 0-(0+0) =0	0 *

Therefore ➜   all opportunity cost are non-negative (i.e. > 0)

Therefore ➜   solution is optimum and there is no

        Scope for further improvement.

Therefore Optimum plan as

X →C(10), X → D(30), X → E(40), Y → A(50), Y → C(50)

Z →B(40), Z → D(10)

Therefore total cost = 10(6) + 30(6) + 40(0) + 50(5) + 50(6) + 40(5) + 10(6)

                = Rs.1050

Step iv)   Therefore above problem

These are two unoccupied cell i.e. **YE and ZE opportunity cost are zero.**

Therefore ➜   it has **multiple optimum solution**

Therefore to obtain alternate solution we can shift some units to these cells as we do it for the cells with highest negative opportunity cost.

(Though the opportunity cost are same XXX cost per unit for the both cell is 0)

A) Draw the closed path **for the cell** (ZE) **(First alternate solution)**

	A	B	C	D	E	Supply
X	7	6	6 (10)	6 (+) (30)	0 (−) (40)	80
Y	5 (50)	7	6 (50)	7	0	100
Z	8	5 (40)	8	6 (10) (−)	0 (+)	50
Demand	50	40	60	40	40	

b) Therefore➔ **alternate transportation plan as →**

	A	B	C	D	E	Supply
X	7	6	6 (10)	6 ☆ (40)	0 ☆ (30)	80
Y	5 (50)	7	6 (50)	7	0	100
Z	8	5 (40)	8	6	0 ☆ (10)	50
Demand	50	40	60	40	40	

Answer from (a) and (b) are **same** with **different transportation plan**.

First **optimum transportation plan as**

X → C(10), X → D(40), X → E(30), Y → A(50), Y → C(50)

Z →B(40), Z → E(0)

With its total cost =   10(6) + 40(6) +30(0) + 50(5) + 50(6) + 40(5) + 10(0)

$$= \quad 1050$$

................................(a)

b)   Draw the closed path for the cost (YE) second alternate solution

	A	B	C	D	E	Supply
X	7	6	6 (+) 10	6 (30)	0 (-) 40	80
Y	50 (50)	7	6 (50) (-)	7	0 (+)	100
Z	8	5 (40)	8	6 (10)	0	50
Demand	50	40	60	40	40	

	A	B	C	D	E	Supply

X	7	6	☆ 6 (50)	6 (30)	0	80
Y	5 (50)	7	☆ 6 (10)	7	☆ 0 (40)	100
Z	8	5 (40)	8	6 (10)	0	50
Demand	50	40	60	40	40	

Second optimum transportation plan as

X →C(50), X → D(30), Y → A(50), Y → C(10)

E(40), Z → B(40), Z → D(10)

With total cost = 50(6) + 30(6) + 50(5) + 10(6) + 40(0) + 40(5) + 10(6)

$$= 1050$$

.................................(b)

C)   CASE OF DEGENRACY:

This is said to be occur when the **number of** independent **occupied cells** (at any solution stage is **less than (m+n-1)**

i)   Degeneracy at the initial solution :

Assign an artificial quantity [(E) epsilon] to one or more unoccupied cell (depending upon the difference in the number of occupied cells and m=n-1) at the independent **position with lower unit cost.**

- E remain in the solution until final solution obtained or degeneracy get resolved / removed.

: E is an infinitesimally small positive quantity so that it does not affect the demand or supply numbers.

ii) **Degeneracy during further stage of solution i.e. in MODI Method**

- This is occur when the reallocation or shifting of units to an unoccupied cell (in MODI Method) **vacates** two or more **occupied cell** simultaneously.

- This is resolve by allocating E to **one or more** of the **recent vacated cells** along the (loosed path, having the lowest unit transportation cost.

- If there is a **tie** assign E arbitrarily.

: Solve the following transportation problem to minimize the total cost.

Origin	Destination			
	D_1	D_2	D_3	Availability
O_1	40	70	90	300
O_2	12	80	30	400
O_3	60	90	45	200
Requirement	300	300	300	

→ Since total supply = total demand

→ It is an balanced transportation cost

Step 1. Using VAM method to find initial feasible solution

origins	D1	D2	D3	Availability	Penallty
O1	40 ⟨300⟩	70	90	300̶, 0	30 ↓
O2	12	80 ⟨100⟩	30 ⟨300⟩	400̶, 100, 0	18, 50̶ 2
O3	60	90 ⟨200⟩	45	200̶, 0	15, 45
Requirements	300̶, 0	╱300 ,200 10	300̶, 0		
Penalty	28	10, 10	15, 15		

Therefore by using 4 allocation entire supply and demand gets fully exhausted.

Therefore   for initial feasible solution total number of
            Allocation for occupied cells   =   4
            m+n-1 = 3+3-1 = 5
Therefore   number of allocation (4) < m+n-1 (5)
Therefore   → Thus **there is a degeneracy case.**

Hence, **we allocate quantity XXXX** to an independent
Unoccupied cell with smallest cost i.e. **to cell O_2O_1**
We draw a closed path for the cell O_2D_1
Reduced matrix become

	D1	D2	D3	Ava
O1	40 ⟨300⟩	70	90	300
O2	★ 12 ⟨∘⟩	80 ⟨100⟩	30 ⟨300⟩	400
O3	60	90 ⟨200⟩	45	200
Req.	300	300	300	

Therefore →**Now**
      Total number of allocation =5
      And m+n-1 = 3+3-1 = 5
Therefore total number of allocation = m+n-1

Hence the solution is feasible

Then we will used **MODI Method** to find

Optimum solution / total cost / Make improvement

Step (ii) Assign and determine row number and column number

( ) using formula (assume)

Step (iii) Use formula

to find

Opportunity cost for **all unoccupied cell.**

Therefore Reduced matrix become

	D1	D2	D3	Ava	Row.No. (ui)
O1	40 30 -	70 38	90 + 32	300	u1=40- 12 =28
O2	12 c	30 100	30 300	400	u2=0
O3	60 38	90 200	45 5	200	u3=90- 80 =10
Req.	300	300	300		
Col.No (vj)	$V_1=12-0$ =12	$V_2=80-0$ =80	V_3-30- 0 =30		

Therefore all the opposite cost are not positive

Opposite cost at O_1D_2 is negative i.e. it is -38

Therefore ➔ Further improvement is required.

⇨ Draw the close path from

the cell with highest.

negative opposite cost i.e. from

the cell O1D$_2$ (see above table)

Therefore ➜ allocate leas cost i.e. 100 to cell O_1D_2.

We get improvement table as

Ist Improvement table

	D1	D2	D3	Ava
O1	40 — 200	70 — 100	90	300
O2	12 — 100	80	30 — 300	400
O3	60	90 — 200	45	200
Req.	300	300	300	

Therefore ➜ It is feasible as, it has 5 occupied

Cell (XXX Here 'XXX' get removed.

Step (iv) Now for above table again we use

MODI Method to (all opposite cost are not the --- it required improvement)

(a) **Finding XXXXXX also find opposite cost (Dij)**

and also all opposite cost are not +ve

therefore draw the close path and make arrangement.

	D1	D2	D3	Ava	Row.No. (ui)
O1	40 (20) −	70 + (100)	90 [32]	300	u1=40−12 =28
O2	+ 12 (100)	80 [38]	30 (300) −	400	u2=0
O3	60 [0]	(−) 90 (200)	45 [−33]	200	u3=90−80 =10
Req.	300	300	300		
Col.No (vj)	V_1=40-0 =40	V_2=70-0 =70	V_3-30-(-28) =58		

Therefore All opposite cost are not positive

Solution is not optimum.

Now select O_3D2 (XXXXXXX= -33) and draw closed

Path, we the shift **200** units along the path.

We get the IInd Improvement solution table as

	D1	D2	D3	Ava
O1	40	70 (300)	90	300
O2	12 (300)	80	30 (100)	400

O3	60	90 ⟨200⟩	45	200
Req.	300	300	300	

IInd Improvement table

Therefore Here number of occupied cell = 4

Which is less than m+n-1 = 5

This happen because of two cells O_1D_1 and O_3D_2

Get **vacated** simultaneously during the allocation of 200 units.

Therefore ➜ **There is a case of degeneracy in MODI Method**

Therefore to resolve it we add XXX **to the recently**

Vacated cell with minimum cost

Therefore cost at O_1D_1 = **40** and cost at D_3D_2 = **90**

Therefore select O_1O_1 and allocate ' ' there solve further using MODI Method.

	D1	D2	D3	Ava	Row.No. (ui)
O1	40 ⟨℮⟩	70 ⟨300⟩	90 ⟨32⟩	300	u1 = 0
O2	12 ⟨300⟩	80 ⟨38⟩	30 ⟨100⟩	400	u2 = -28

03	60	90	45	200	u3 = -13
	23	33	⟨200⟩		
Req.	300	300	300		
Col.No (vj)	$V_1 = 40$	$V_2 = 70$	$V_3 = 58$		

As all the opposite cost (   ) are positive.

Therefore → solution is optimum and there is no scope for

Further improvement

Also number of allocation = 5= m+n-1 (5)

Hence, solution is feasible also.

Thus the transaction plan is

O1 →D2(300), O2 →D1(300), O2 → D3(100)

O3 → D3 (200)

Therefore XXX being an artificially small quantity, **it is ignore**

Therefore Total cost   = 300(70) + 300 (12) + 100(30) + 200 (45)

= **36,600** required answer.

D.   Maximization problem :

Transportation problem method can be used for a maximization problem, by covering it into an equivalent minimization problem.

- Locate the largest per unit profit figure in the table and subtract all profit figures from it to get an equivalent relative loss matrix.

- Solve further as a normal transportation problem to get the optimum solution table.

:

Solve the following T.P. to maximize profit and give he criteria for optimality.

Origin	Destination				Supply
	1	2	3	4	
A	40	25	22	33	100
B	44	35	30	30	30
C	38	38	28	33	70
Demand	40	20	60	30	

Therefore total cost   =   10(4) + 10(22) + 30(11) + 50(44) + 30(0)

+ 20(0) + 50(16)

=   **3710/-**

Using MODI Method

Answer – 3710/-

Chapter III

Sequencing Models and Related Problems

Introduction

The sequencing problems involves the determination of an optimal order or sequence and performing a series and jobs by a number of facilities (that are arranged in specific order) so as to optimize the total time or cost.

Sequencing problems may be classified in two groups:

I   In the first group, there are 'n' different jobs to be performed. Where each job requires processing on some or all and 'm' different types of machines.

Where the order in which these machines are used for processing each job. [For example > Each jobs is to be processed first on machine 'A', then on machine 'B', then on machine 'c' i.e. order is ABC] is given.

Also there is expected or actual processing time for each job on each machine is known.

  If there are 4 jobs to be processed on each of the 5 machines (i.e. n=4 and m=5), the total number of *theoretically* possible different sequences will be $(4!)^5$ That is $(n!)^m$.

II In 2nd group of problems deals with <u>Job shops</u> having a number of machines and a list of task to be performed.

Each time a task is completed by a machine, the next task to start on it has get decided.

Thus the list of task will changes as fresh order is received.

SEQUENCING PROBLEMS:

In sequencing problems, there are two or more customers to be secured (or jobs to be done) and one or more facilities(machines)are available for this purpose.

Sequencing problems have been most commonly encountered in 'production shops' where different products are to be processed over various combinations of machines.

Since the <u>total **elapsed time**</u> (also called makes pan) is fixed and **equal to the sum of processing times for all jobs** for all its sequences.

Following are the **various optimality criteria** –

- Minimizing the total elapsed time.

- Minimizing the mean flow time.

- Minimizing the idle time of machine.

- **Minimizing total tardiness** :

- Lateness of a job is defined as the Difference between the actual completion time of the job and its due date.

If **lateness is positive**, it is termed as **tardiness**.

Total tardiness is the sum of tardiness over all the jobs in the set.

- Minimizing number of tardy jobs.

- Minimize in process inventory cost.

- Minimize the cost of being late.

General sequence problem may be defined as follow.

Let there are **'n' jobs** (1,2,3,....n) each of these has to be process, one at a time, on each of the **'m' machines** (A,B,C,.....)

Symbolically

Let A_i = time required for job 'i' on machine 'A'

   B_i = time required for job 'i' on machine 'B'

etc...................

and   T = Total elapsed time for jobs 1,2, ...,n
i.e. it is the time from start of the
first job the completion of the last job.

The problem is to determine sequence (i_1, i_2, ... i_n) where, (2_1, 2_2, ... 2_n) is a permutation / arrangement of integrs (1, 2, ... n) (jobs) to minimize the Time 'T'

**   Analectic method have been developed to slove five simple cases.

XXXXXX

1. 'n' jobs and one machine 'A'

2. 'n' jobs and two machines 'A' and 'B'

3. 'n' jobs and three machines 'A' , 'B' and 'C'

4. two jobs and 'm' machines.

5. 'n' jobs and 'm' machines.

** Assumption in sequencing problems.

i. Only one operation is carried out on a machine at a particular time.

ii. Each operation, once started must be completed

iii. An operation must be completed before its succeeding operation can start.

iv. Only one machine of each type is available.

v. A job is processed as soon as possible, but only in the order specified.

vi. The transportation time i.e. the time required to transfer jobs from one machine to another machine is negligible.

vii. Jobs are completely known.

** PROCESSING of 'n' jobs THROUGH ONE MACHINE

The case when a number of jobs is to be processed an a single facility is quite common in actual practice.

e.g. - Number of patient waiting for doctor.

- Number of program waiting for computer.

- Number of cases to be solved at a service station.

- Number of different breakdown machines to be repaired by machine etc.

Static job The job is a static in the sensethat any new job that arrives does not disturb the processing of 'n' jobs.

Therefore = new job arrivals **wait** for being considered in the next batch of jobs after the processing of the current 'n' jobs is completed.

Let 'n' = number of different jobs.
E_i = Processing time of job 'i'
W_i = Waiting time (before processing) for job i
F_i = Flow time of job i

$$F_i = W_i + t_i$$

C_i = Completion time of job i
d_i = due date of job i
L_i = Lateness of job i

$$L_i = C_i + d_i$$

E_i = Earliness of job
T_i = Tardiness of job $\boxed{E_i = d_i + C_i}$
NT = Number of tardy jobs.

*Shortest processing Time (SPT) Rule.

a. Sequencing the jobs in a way that the job with least processing time is picked up first, followed by the one with the next smallest processing time and also so on is known as SPT sequencing and it achieves the following objective.

- minimize the mean waiting time.

- minimize the mean flow time.

- minimize mean lateness.

- minimize the mean number of jobs waiting as in-process inventory.

b. In case importance of the jobs varies, a weight 'wi' is assigned to each job, a larger value indicating greater importance.

The weighted mean Flow Time

$$WMFT = \frac{\sum\limits_{i=1}^{n} WiFi}{\sum\limits_{i=1}^{m} Wi}$$

This rule is called **Weighted Shortest processing time (WSPT) rule.**

Example I

1. Six jobs A, B, C, D, E, and F have arrived at one time to be processed on a single machine Assuming that no new jobs arrive thereafter determine.

Job	:	A	B	C	D	E	F
Processing Time (Minutes)	:	7	6	8	4	3	5

Determine i) Optimal sequence as per SPT rule.

ii) Completion times of the jobs.

iii) Mean flow time.

IV) Average in-process inventory.

i) As per shortest processing time rule (SPT)

Optimal sequence is

E - D - F - B - A - C

ii) Completing times of the jobs are

3, 7, 12, 18, 25 and 33 minutes respectively

iii) Mean flow time is

$$\frac{3+7+12+18+25+33}{6} = \frac{98}{6} = \frac{49}{3}$$

$$= \underline{\textbf{16.33 min}}$$

Example II

Eight jobs 1,2,3, ..., 8 are to be processed on a **single machine**. The processing times, due dates and importance weights of the jobs are represented in table

Li = ci-di	Ci	Job	Processing time ti (minutes)		Due date di (minutes)	Importance Weight (Wi)	ti / Wi
-4	11	1	5	3	15	1	5.0
22	32	2	8	6	10	2	4.0
2	17	3	6	4	15	3	2.0
-22	3	4	3	1	25	1	3.0
22	42	5	10	7	20	2	5.0
16	6	6	14	8	40	3	4.7
-21	24	7	7	5	45	2	3.5
-44	6	8	3	2	50	1	3.0

Assuming that no new jobs arrive thereafter, determine using **SPT rule** and **WSPT rule find**

    i)   Optimal sequence.

    ii)   Completion time of these jobs.

    iii)   Mean flow time as well as Weighted mean flow Time.

    iv)   Average in-process inventory.

    v)   Lateness, mean lateness and maximum lateness.

    vi)   Number of jobs actually late.

***

I]   As per SPT rule:-

    i.   optimal sequence is

        4 – 8 -1 – 3 -7 – 2 – 5 - 6

ii] Completion times of these jobs are (I)

3, 6, 11, 17, 24, 32, 42 and 56 minutes **respectively**

iii] **Mean flow time**

$$\frac{\frac{3+6+11+17+24+32+42+5}{6}}{8} = \frac{191}{8}$$

= 23.875 minutes

iv] **Average in process inventory**

Since,

Initially number of jobs waiting as in process inventory

Are 8 during the time 0-3 minutes, similarly

7 during the time 3-6 minutes

6 during the time 6-11 minutes

5 during the time 11-17 minutes

4 during the time 17-24 minutes

3 during the time 24-32 minutes

2 during the time 32-42 minutes

1during the time 42-56 minutes

Therefore Average in process inventory =

$$\frac{(8\times3)+(7\times3)+(6\times5)+(5\times6)+(4+7)+(3\times8)+(2+10)+(1\times14)}{3+3+5+6+7+8+10+14} = \frac{191}{56}$$

= 3.41 jobs

v] **Lateness mean Lateness and maximum lateness**

First find lateness of various jobs

by formula

$$L_i = C_i + d_i$$

Computation time of Various job   due date (Given)

(calculated in <u>step ii</u>)

Job no	1	2	3	4	5	6	7	8
Computation time (i)	11	32	17	3	42	56	26	6
Lateness (Li = (i-di)	-4	22	2	- 22	22	16	- 21	- 44
Computation due date (Given)	15	10	15	25	20	40	45	50

*** Mean Lateness   =

$$\frac{-4+22+2+22+22+16-21-44}{8} \qquad = \qquad \frac{-29}{8}$$

=   3.625 minutes

*** **Maximum Lateness** = 22 min   (maximum +ve)

vi]   Number of jobs actually late

= 4   (+ve lateness)

II]   **As per WSPT rule :**

i)   **Optimal sequence** is

Therefore as per the calculation of it optimal sequence of job is

$$3 - 4 - 8 - 7 - 2 - 6 - 1 - 5$$

ii) **Completion Time of these jobs are** (i)

$$6 - 9 - 12 - 19 - 27 - 41 - 46 - 56$$

iii) (a) **Mean flow time**

$$\frac{6+9+12+19+27+41+46+56}{8}$$

$$= 27 \text{ minutes}$$

(b) Weighted mean flow time = XXXXX

$$\frac{(3\times6)+(1\times9)+(1\times12)+(2\times19)+(2+19)+(2\times27)+(3+41)+(1\times46)+(2\times56)}{3+1+1+2+2+3+1+2} = \frac{412}{15}$$

$$= 24.47 \text{ min}$$

iv) **Average In process Inventory**

Initially number of jobs waiting as in process inventory

are '8' during the 0–6 minutes

'7' during the 6–9 minutes

'6' during the 9–12 minutes

'5' during the 12–19 minutes sequence

'4' during the 19–27 minutes

'3' during the 27–41 minutes

'2' during the 41–46 minutes

'1' during the 46–56 minutes

As per new job

after calculating of

$(t_i + w_i)$

Therefore Average In process Inventory

$$\frac{(8\times6)+(7\times3)+(6\times3)+(5\times7)+(4+8)+(3\times14)+(2\times5)+(1\times10)}{6+3++7+8+14+5+10} = \frac{216}{56}$$

=3.86 Jobs

v) **Lateness, mean Lateness and maximum lateness**

Find lateness of the job – 1 to job – 8

by formula $\boxed{L_i = C_i + d_i}$

That is

Job	1	2	3	4	5	6	7	8
Lateness $(C_i + d_i)$	31	17	-9	-16	36	1	-26	-38

Therefore

Mean Lateness

$$= \frac{31+17-9-16+36+1+26-38}{} = \underline{-4}$$

$$= \frac{8}{-0.5 \text{ minutes}} \qquad \qquad 8$$

Maximum lateness = 36 min (maximum +ve value)

vi)   Number of jobs actually late = 4 (total +ve lateness)

III]

Earliest Due Date (EDD) rule

"According to this rule **jobs are sequenced** in the **order** of **non-decreasing due dates**."

This rule minimizes the maximum job lateness as well as maximum job tardiness.

However, this rule tends to make more jobs tardy and increase the **mean tardiness.**

Same above example

Example

by EDD rule

Eight jobs 1, 2, 3, ..., 8 are to be processed on a single machine. The processing times, due dates and importance weight of the jobs are given below.

Completion Time	Job	Processing time (t_i)min	Due date d_i (min)		Lateness L_i (min)
13	1	5	15	2	-2
8	2	8	10	1	-2
19	3	6	15	3	4
32	4	3	25	5	7

29	5	10	20	4	9
46	6	14	4	6	6
53	7	7	45	7	8
56	8	3	50	8	6

Find

i) Optimal sequence as per EDD rule.

ii) Completion time of the job.

iii) Mean flow time.

iv) Average in process inventory.

v) Lateness, mean lateness and maximum lateness of the job.

vi) Number of jobs actually late.

Using EDD rule

Solution   by Earliest Due date rule

(i)   Optimal job sequence is

2- 1- 3 – 5 - 4 -6 -7 – 8

(ii)   Completion time of these jobs are

C_i = 8 – 13 – 19 – 29 -32 – 46 -53 – 56

Minutes

respelly

(iii)   Mean flow time

$$= \frac{8+13+19+29+32+46+53+56}{8} = \frac{256}{8}$$

$$= \underline{32 \text{ minutes}}$$

(iv)   **Average in process inventory**

Since initially number of jobs waiting as in process inventory

are8 during the 0–8 minutes, simily

7 during the 8–13 minutes

6 during the 13–119 minutes

5 during the 19 – 29 minutes

4 during the 29 – 32 minutes

3 during the 32– 46 minutes

2 during the 46– 53 minutes

1 during the 53–56 minutes

Therefore Average In process Inventory

$$\frac{(8\times8)+(7\times5)+(6\times6)+(5\times10)+(4+3)+(3\times14)+(2\times7)+(1\times3)}{6+3++7+8+14+5+10} \quad = \quad \frac{256}{26}$$

= 4.57 Jobs

(V) Lateness of the various jobs (L_i = C_i – d_i)

Job number	1	2	3	4	5	6	7	8
Completion time (C_i)	13	8	19	32	29	46	53	56
due date (d_i)	15	10	15	25	20	40	45	50

Lateness Li = (Ci + di)	-2	-2	4	7	9	6	8	6

Mean Lateness

$$= \frac{-2-2+4+7+9+6+8+6}{8} \qquad = \qquad \frac{36}{8}$$

Maximum Lateness   = 9 minutes

(v)   Number of jobs actually

Late   = 6 (Total number of +ve L_i)

Thus EDD rule, Reduces the maximum lateness
from 22 minutes to 9 minutes
However it has increased the mean lateness
from -3.625minutesto 4.5 minutes
Also number of late jobs has increased from 4 to 6

IV]   ## Slack Time Remaining (STR) Rule

"Slack Time for a job is defined as the due date of the job minus its processing time."

"Sequencing the jobs in such a way's that the jobs with the least slack time are picked up first for processing, followed by the one with the next smallest slack time and so on is called the slack time remaining (STR) rule."

Example

The information regarding jobs to be schedule of through one machine is given below.

Job	:	A	B	C	D	E	F	G
Processing Time (days)	:	4	12	2	11	10	3	6
Due date (days)	:	20	30	15	16	18	5	9

1. What is the first come, first serves (FCFS) schedule?

2. What is the shortest Processing Time (STP) schedule?

3. What is the Black Time remaining schedule?

4. What is the earliest due date schedule?

5. What are the mean flow times for each of the schedule above?

(1)   First come first schedule

FSFS schedule is

A →B →C →D →E →F

And the processing times will be as follows.

Jobs	Machine	
	In time	Out time
A	8	4
B	4	16
C	16	18
D	18	29
E	29	39
F	39	42
G	42	48

(2)   Shortest Processing Time (SPT) schedule

SPT schedule is

C → F → A → G → E → D → B

And the processing times will be as follows

Jobs	Machine	
	In time	Out time
C	0	2
F	2	5
A	5	9
G	9	15
E	15	25
D	25	36
B		

(3)   Slack Time remaining schedule

First calculate the slack time for each job as

Job	Processing time t_i (days)	Due date d_i (Days)	Slack Time days ($d_i - t_i$)	New Job
A	4	20	16	6
B	12	30	18	7
C	2	15	13	5
D	11	16	5	3
E	10	18	8	4
F	3	5	2	1
G	6	9	3	2

Therefore per **STR** rule schedule is

F → G → B → E → C → A → B

and

Processing time will be

Jobs	Machine	
	In time	Out time
F	0	3
G	3	9
D	9	20
E	20	30
C	30	32
A	32	36
B	36	48

(4) **Earliest due date (EDD) schedule**

As per EDD rule, schedule is

F → G → C → D → E → A → B

and the Processing time will be

Jobs	Machine	
	In time	Out time
F	0	3
G	3	9
C	9	11
B	11	22
E	22	32
A	32	36

B	36	48

(5) Mean Flow Time

(a) FCFS Schedule

mean flow time =

$$= \frac{4+16+18+29+39+42+48}{7} = \frac{196}{7} = 28 \text{ days}$$

(b) SPT Schedule

mean flow time =

$$= \frac{2+5+9+15+25+36+48}{7} = \frac{140}{7} = 20 \text{ days}$$

(C) STR Schedule

mean flow time =

$$= \frac{3+9+20+30+32+36+48}{7} = \frac{178}{7} = 25.43 \text{ days}$$

(d) EDD Schedule

mean flow time =

$$= \frac{33+9+11+22+32+36+48}{7} = \frac{161}{7} = 23 \text{ days}$$

Processing 'n' Jobs Through Two Machines

There are 'n' different jobs to be processed on two machines and it is desired to determine the optimal sequence of jobs that minimizes T, the total elapsed time from the stock of the first job on first machine to the completion of the last job on second machine.

Total elapsed time includes idle time, if any of the following condition assumed.

1. Only two machines are involved A & B.

2. Each job is processed in the order AB.

3. Cost in process inventory is either same for each job or is too small to be considered.

4. Order of completion of jobs has no significance.

5. The actual / expected processing times A_1, A_2., ... A_n & B_1, B_2,

Job 'i'	Machine 'A'	Machine 'B'
1	A_1	B_1
2	A_2	B_2
3	A_3	B_3
.	.	.
.	.	.
.	A_i	B_i
.	.	.
N	A_n	B_n

........B_n are known.

Steps to solve the 'n' jobs – two machine

Step 1. Examine the columns of processing times on machine 'A' and machine 'B' and **find the smallest value [Min (A,B)]**

Step 2.

If this value falls in **column A**, schedule this job **first on machine A**

If this value falls in **column B**, schedule this job **last on machine A**

(Therefore the given order AB)

If those are equal minimal values (there is **tie**) one in each column, **schedule** the one in the first column **first on machine A**; **and** the one in the second column, **last on machine A**

If **both equal values** are in the **first column (A)**, select the one with **lowest entry** in **column 'B' first**

If both equal values are in the **second column (B)**, select the one with the lowest entry in **column 'A' first**

Step 3.

Cross out the job assigned and continue the process (repeat step 1 and step 2, placing one jobs **next** to **first** or next to last till all the jobs are schedule. The resulting sequence will **Minimize T**.

Example

A machine operator has to perform two operations **turning** and **threading**, on a number of different jobs. The time required to perform these operations (in minutes) for each job is known Determine the order in which the jobs should be processed in order to minimize the total time required to turn out all the jobs.

Job	Time for turning (min) i.e. machine A	Time for threading (min) i.e. machine B
1	3	8

2	12	10
3	5	9
4	2	6
5	9	3
6	11	1

Also, find the total processing time and idle time for turning and threading operations.

Solution   :   By examining the columns,

We find the smallest value, it is

Threading time of 1 min for job – 6

In second column.

Therefore   Thus we schedule job – 6 last for turning as shown below

					6

Cross out the 6th job assignment and continue

Therefore reduced set of processing times becomes.

Job	Turning time (min)	Threading time (min)
1	3	8
2	12	10
3	5	9
4	2	6
5	9	3

Now, again smallest value is turning time of 2 min for job – 4 in first column.

Therefore - We schedule job – 4 first as shown below

4					6

Again **reduced set of processing times becomes**

Job	Turning time (min)	Threading time (min)
1	3	8
2	12	10
3	5	9
5	9	3

Therefore - There are two equal minimal values:

i.e. turning time of 3 min for job-1 in I^{st} column and threading time of 3 min for job-5 in IInd column.

Therefore - Acc/ to rule

Job-1 schedule next ot job 4 and job-5 next to job-6 as show

4	1			5	6

Again reduced set of processing times becomes

Job	Turning time	Threading time
2	12	10
3	5	9

Therefore - the smallest value is turning time of 5 min. for job 3 belongs to 1st column

Therefore - We schedule job 3, next ot job 1 and we get **optimal sequence** as

4	1	3	2	5	6

Now, we calculate the **elapsed time corresponding** to the **optimal sequence** as

Operation job sequence	Turning operation (A)		Threading operation (B)		Idle time machine
	In time	Out time	In time	Out time	
4	0	2	2	8	2
1	2	5	8	16	0
3	5	10	16	25	0
2	10	22	25	35	0
5	22	31	35	38	0
6	31	42	42	**43**	4

Thus, the minimum elapsed time is **43** min

Idle time for turning operation is(43-42) = **1** min

&Idle time for threading operation is

$(2+0+0+0+0+4)=$ **6** min

- There are seven jobs, each of which has to go through the machine-A and B in order AB processing time in hours are given as

Job   :   1   2   3   4   5   6   7
Machine – A   :   3   12   15   6   10   11   9

Machine – B   :   8   10   10   6   12   **1**   3

By examining the processing times, we find the smallest value. **It is 1 hour for job 6 on machine B.**

Thus we schedule **job-6** last on machine-A

					6

Therefore reduced set of processing times becomes

Job   :   1   2   3   4   5   7

Machine – A   :   **3**   12   15   6   10   9

Machine – B   :   8   10   10   6   12   **3**

Thus, job 1 is scheduled first and job 7 next to job 6 as shown below

1				7	6

Therefore reduced set of processing time becomes

Job   :   2   3   4   5

Machine – A   :   12   15   **6**   10

Machine – B   :   10   10   **6**   12

Again there are **two** equal minimal values:

Processing time of 6-hours for job-4 on machine-A

As well as on machine – B

Therefore schedule becomes

1	4			7	6

OR

1			4	7	6

Therefore reduced set of processing time becomes

Job   :   2   3   5

Machine – A   :   12   15   10

Machine – B   :   10   10   12

Again there are three equal minimal values

Processing time 10 hours for job-5 on machine-A and for job-2 and job-3 on machine-B

Therefore - selected job-5 on machine- A

Therefore schedule becomes

| 1 | 4 | 5 | | | 7 | 6 | **OR** | 1 | 5 | | | 4 | 7 | 6 |

Therefore reduced set of promise time becomes

Job   :   2   3
Machine – A :   12   15
Machine – B :   10   10

Again there are **two** equal minimal values.

Processing time 10 hours for job-2 and job-3 for the **same** machine – B.

Therefore rule,

Both the same value in 2nd column

Select one with lowest entry in column 'A' first

Select job – E first (process time in column A = 12)

New job sequence is

| 1 | 4 | 5 | 3 | 2 | 7 | 6 |

OR

| 1 | 5 | 3 | 2 | 4 | 7 | 6 |

Now, we can calculate the elapsed time corresponding to **either of** the optimal sequences, using individual processing times given in the problem.

> Note
>
> **Since**, the elapsed time and idle times for machine 'A' and machine 'B' will be **same for either sequence.**

Therefore the details corresponding to 1st schedule are as :-

Consider 1st optimal job sequence

job	Machine(A)		Machine (B)		Idle time for machine B
	Time in	Time Out	Time in	Time Out	
1	0	3	3	11	3
4	3	9	11	17	0
5	9	**19**	**19**	31	2
3	19	34	34	44	3
2	34	46	46	**56**	2
7	49	**55**	**56**	59	0
6	55	**66**	66	**67**	7

Therefore, Minimum Elapsed time – 67 hours

Idle time for machine 'A' = 67-66= 1 min   &

Idle time for machine 'B' = 3+0+2+3+2+0+7= 17 min

A refrigeration company has six plants located in different parts of a city. Every year it is necessary for each plant to be completely overhauled, the overhauling is carried out in two stages 'A' and 'B' and each stage requires a crew of workmen with completely different skills. The work on stage 'B' can start only when stage 'A' has been completed. The plant has to be closed for the entire period of the overhauling. The company, at present is following the schedule of the overhaul of the six plants as given below.

Time required by the crew (days)

Plant	:	P_1	P_2	P_3	P_4	P_5	P_6
Crew A	:	12	9	10	8	10	10
Crew B	:	10	7	9	14	6	8

Find

1. Determine the optimal sequence

2. If down time of any of the six plants cost Rs.5,000 per day, idle time for crew 'A' costs Rs.1,500 per day and idle time for crew 'B' cost Rs.2,500 per day, which of the two schedule the present one or the one determined in partly will be more economical?

   What are their respective costs?

Solution :-

i.e. we have to calculate total cost for

        i)   present schedule (Given)

        ii)   Optimal schedule (To be find)

   i)   For Present schedule

Calculate the Down time of the plants and idle time in days for Crew – a and Crew – B as –

Plants	Crew A		Crew B		Down time	Idle time	
	Start	Finish	Start	Finish		Crew A	Crew
P_1	0	12	12	22	22	-	12

P$_2$	12	21	22	29	17	-	-
P$_3$	21	31	31	40	19	-	2
P$_4$	31	39	40	54	23	-	-
P$_5$	39	49	54	60	21	-	-
P$_6$	49	59	60	68	19	9	-
Total					**121**	**9**	**14**

Since Given that

Down time of six plant cost Rs.5,000 per day

Idle time for Crew – A cost Rs.1,500 per day

Idle time for Crew – B cost Rs.2,500 per day

Therefore

Total Cost =

$$= \quad Rs.6,53,500/- \qquad .... (I)$$

ii) First find the optimal plants schedule by Johnson & Beuman rule and that are

| P$_4$ | P$_1$ | P$_3$ | P$_6$ | P$_2$ | P$_5$ |

Then calculate the down time of the plants for optimal schedule and idle time in days for crew – A and Crew – B as –

Plants	Crew A		Crew B		Down time	Idle time	
	Start	Finish	Start	Finish		Crew A	Crew
P$_4$	0	8	8	22	22	-	8

P_1	8	20	22	32	24	-	-
P_3	20	30	32	41	21	-	-
P_6	30	40	41	49	19	-	-
P_2	40	49	49	56	16	-	-
P_5	49	59	59	65	16	6	3
Total					**118**	**6**	**11**

Therefore

    Total cost =

          =   Rs.6,26,500/-   .... (II)

Therefore From (I) and (II)

    Optimal sequence, total cost is less

Therefore optimal sequence is more economical as it reduces the cost by **Rs.27,000/-**

(4)   A manufacturing company processes 6 different jobs on two machines A and B. Number of units of each job and its processing items on A and B are given in table

Find the **optimal sequence**

   - total minimum elapsed time

     and idle time for either machine

Job No.	No. of units of each job	Processing time	
		Machine – A (min)	Machine – B (min)
1	3	5	8
2	4	16	7

3	2	6	11
4	5	3	5
5	2	9	7.5
6	3	6	14

Solution:-

Therefore by Johnson & Beumen rule

4	1	3	6	5	2
		5	3	2	3

                                                        2   4

Number of units   -

Therefore -   4th number jobs having 5 numbers of units

                    1st number jobs having 3 numbers of units

                    3rd number jobs having 2 numbers of units

                    6th number jobs having 3 numbers of units

                    5th number jobs having 2 numbers of units

                    2nd number jobs having 4 numbers of units

Now, we conclude the table to determine the total elapsed time

Job No.	Unit no of the job	Machine A		Machine B		Idle time of machine-B in (min)
		Time in (min)	Time out (min)	Time in (min)	Time out (min)	
4	1st	0	3	3	8	3
	2nd	3	6	8	13	-
	3rd	6	9	13	18	-
	4th	9	12	18	23	-
	5th	12	15	23	28	-
1	1st	15	20	28	36	-
	2nd	20	25	36	44	-
	3rd	25	30	44	52	-
3	1st	30	36	52	63	-
	2nd	36	42	63	74	-
6	1st	42	48	74	88	-
	2nd	48	54	88	102	-
	3rd	54	60	102	116	-
5	1st	60	69	116	123.5	-
	2nd	69	78	123.5	131	-
2	1st	78	94	131	138	-
	2nd	94	110	138	145	-
	3rd	110	126	145	152	-

	4th	126	142	152	**159**	-

Therefore from the table

Total elapsed time (minimum) is **159** min

& idle time for machine A is (159-142 = **17** min)

& idle time for machine B is **3** min

Chapter IV

COST COMPONENT OF INVENTORY

An inventory consists of usable but idle resources such a men, machine, material and money.

When resources involved as a material the inventory is called as "SOTCK"

There are four costs considered in inventory control models.
I.   Purchase cost.

II.   Inventory carrying or stock holding cost.

III.   Procurement cost of setup cost.

IV.   Shortage cost (due to disservice of cost)

I.   Purchase Cost :

       It is the price that paid for purchasing or producing an item.

       It may be constant per unit or may vary with the quantity purchased / produced.

       If the cost per unit is constant, it does not affect the Inventory control decision.

       However, the purchase cost if defiantly considered when it varies as in quality discount situation.

II.   Inventory carrying or stock holding cost :

       It arises on account of stock holding cost. Stock and interest rate paid on capital tied up with the stock.

They vary directly with the size of inventory as well as the time for which the item it held in stock.

Various component of stockholding cost are,

a. Cost of Money :

It is important component.

It is capital tied up in inventories. It is generally taken around 15% to 20% value of investment.

b. Cost of storage space:

It consists of rent for space, heating, lighting and there atmosphere control expenses.

Typical values may vary from 1 to 3%.

c. Depreciation and deterioration cost :

Deterioration = Weaking

They are especially important for fashion item or item undergoing chemical changes during stock. Also, crockery are liable to damage, breakage 0.2. % to 1% of the stock value may be lost due to damage and deterioration.

d. Obsolescence cost :

It depends upon the nature of item in stock electric and computer component are likely to be fast outdated.

Changes in design also lead to obsolescence

It may be taken 5% of stock value.

e. Taxes and Insurance :

Most organization has insurance over against possible loss from theft, fire etc.

It may cost 1% to 2% of invested capital.

f. Handling cost :

These include all costs associated with the movement of stock.

Such as cost of labour, overhead crane and other machinery used for its purchase.

g. Record keeping and administrative cost :

This is no use of keeping stocks unless one can easily know whether or not required item is in stock.

This is signifies the need for record keeping and administration.

III. Procurement cost or set up cost :'

These include the fixed cost associated with placing of an order or setting up machinery before starting production.

They include cost of purchase, requisition follow up, receiving the goods, quality control, cost of mailing, telephone cost and other follow up actions, accounting, auditing etc.

Also called as order cost or replenishment cost. They are assumed to be independent of the quantity ordered or produced.

But directly proportional to the number of orders placed.

IV. Shortage cost :

These costs are associated with either a delay in meeting demands or the inability to meet.

It includes the cost of loss of goodwill and cost of idle equipment, quantity in short.

Chapter V

INVENTORY THEORY

Q. Describe inventory model without shortage.

Inventory means stock

5000 KG.

C – Price / Purchase cost of their item in Rs....
D – Annual demand.
C_o- Ordering cost (Rs./Order)

This includes the cost to place an order. It is also known as, procurement / Replenishment cost.

Ch: Holding cost or inventory carrying the cost required to maintain the stock (inventory) - also known as Inventory carrying cost.
T: Optimal order cycle

(When we should order)
(Time between two orders)
N= number of order in given period of time
Eoq = Economic order quantity.
It gives the number of unit which is ordered to minimize the total inventory cost of maximize the profit.

$$(Lot\ Size)\colon EOQ\ (Q^*) = \sqrt{\frac{2DCo}{Ch}}$$

Order cycle time $=T=\sqrt{\dfrac{2DCo}{Ch}}$

Number of orders $\quad\quad\quad\quad$ N=1/t
TVC=Total (minimal) Variable Inventory Cost.
TVC=$\sqrt{2DCoCh}$

TC= Total (average) Inventory Cost.
TC=DVC+TVC
TC=DC+$\sqrt{2DCoCh}$

Shortage: Incomplete stock.

Example: 1

A manufacturer has to supply his customer 600 units of his product per year shortages are not allowed. Inventors carrying cost amount of Rs. 0.60 unit / year.
Set up cost per run is Rs. 80
Find

   i.   Economic order quantity.

   ii.   Minimum yearly cost.

   iii. Optimal period of supply per order

   iv. How may orders can be placed?

Given,
Annual demand p=600 unit / year.
Ch = Inventory carrying cost. = 0.60 / year
(i.e 1 unit to place in stock 60 paisa require per)
Co=80 per Order

   i.   Economic order quantity.

$$EoQ=\sqrt{\frac{2DCo}{Ch}}$$

$$=\sqrt{\frac{2x80x600}{0.60}}=\sqrt{\frac{160x600}{0.60}}=\sqrt{\frac{96000}{0.60}}$$

$$=\sqrt{160000}=400$$

   ii.   Mininum yearly cost

$$TVC=\sqrt{2.D.Co.Ch}$$
$$=\sqrt{2.600 \times 80 \times 0.60}$$
$$=240$$

iii Optimal period of supply per order.

$$t=\sqrt{\frac{2Co}{DCh}}=\sqrt{\frac{2.80}{600.0.60}}=\sqrt{\frac{160}{360}}=\sqrt{\frac{16}{36}}=\frac{9}{6}$$

$$t=\frac{9}{6}/year$$

$$\therefore \frac{2}{3 \times 12(month)} = 8$$

iv   Number of order

$$n=\frac{1}{t}$$

$$=\frac{1}{2/3}=3/2$$

$$n=1.5$$

$$n\cong 1$$

Example: 2

Determine   EOQ   from   following   dates   Ordering   cost 200/order,carrying cost   20% of the unit cost per year,

Unit cost is 25 Rs.

Annual requirement if Rs. 50,000/-

I.   If annual requirement becomes 4 times the current, would the EOQ become 4 times the current one ? why?

D = 50,000/- Rs. Is annual demand ordering cost Co =200 per order carrying cost Ch = 20% of unit cost.

($\therefore$ i.e 5/- Rs. Cost require go place 1/- Rs. Inventory.

C = Rs. 25/-

$$EOQ = Q^* = \sqrt{\frac{2.D.Co}{Ch}}$$

$$= \sqrt{\frac{2 \times 5000 \times 200}{5}} \qquad = \sqrt{400000} = 2000$$

$4XD = 4 \times 50000 - 200000$ Rs

$$4 \times EoQ = \sqrt{\frac{2.D.Co}{Ch}}$$

$$= \sqrt{\frac{2 \times 200000 \times 200}{5}}$$

$$= 4000$$

When D = 50000

∴ EOQ = 2000

When D = 200000

EoQ = 4000

The data available gives economic order quality does not vary with the demand in proportion 1:1.

Example: 3

The production department for a company requires 3600 kg. of raw material. For manufacturing a particular product per year.

It has been estimated that the cost of placing an order is Rs.36

The cost of carrying inventory is 25% of the investment in the inventories.

The price is Rs.10 per kg.

The purchase manger wish to determine an ordering policy for raw material.

Advice him to find

   i.   Optional lot size

   ii.   Optimal order cycle time.

   iii. Number of orders.

   iv. Minimum yearly inventory cost.

D = 3600 kg / year

3600kg

Co = 36 Rs. Per order

C_h = 25% of investment inventories

C = 10/- Rs. Per kg (Rs / Unit / Unit time that is year)

$$\therefore C_h = \frac{25}{100} \times 10$$

C_h = 2.5 Rs/Kg/year.

I.   Optimal lot size = EoQ

$$EoQ = \sqrt{\frac{2.D.Co}{Ch}}$$

$$= \sqrt{\frac{2.3600.36}{2.5}} = \sqrt{\frac{259200}{2.5}} = 103680$$

= 321.99 Kg

II.   Optimal order cycle time.

$$t = \sqrt{\frac{2.Co}{D.Ch}} = \sqrt{\frac{2 \times 36}{3600 \times 2.5}}$$

$$t = \sqrt{\frac{72}{9000}} = 0.08944 \text{ year}$$

$\therefore$ t = 1.07 month

III.   Number of order = $\frac{1}{t}$

$$\frac{1}{=0.08944} = 11.23 \text{ i.e} \approx 11 \, per \, ord.$$

IV.   Minimum yearly inventory cost.

$$\text{TVC} = \sqrt{2.D.Co.Ch}$$
$$= \sqrt{2 \times 3600 \times 36 \times 2.5}$$
$$= 804.98$$

Exercise   entory model,
  1.   Classical model

  2. Non- uniform rate of demand. (Shortage are not allowed)

Example: 4

  A stockage has to supply 400 unit of product every Monday to his customer
  He gets a product at Rs.50/- per unit from the manufacturer. The cost of ordering
  and transportation from the manufacturer is Rs.75/- per order. The cost of
  carrying inventory is 7.5% per year of the cost of the product. Find

  i.   Economic lot size.

  ii.   The total optimal cost (including capital cost)

  iii. The total weekly profit if the item sold for 55/- per unit.

Given,
D = 400 x 52 (week per years)
C = 20,800
C = 50 kg.
C_h= 7.5 % of cost of product
C_o = 75 per order

i. $EoQ = \sqrt{\dfrac{2.Co}{D.Ch}}$

$= \sqrt{\dfrac{20.800 \times 75}{0.072}}$

$= \sqrt{\dfrac{60000}{0.072}} = 912.87$

iii. The total optimal cost (including capital cost)

TC =DVC+TVC
$TVC = \sqrt{2.D.Co.Ch}$
$TVC = \sqrt{2 \times 400 \times 75 \times 0.072}$
TVC=65.726
TC=400 $\times 50 + 65.725$
=20000+65.725
=20065.725 Rs.

iii.   Total profit if item sold at 55 per unit.
∴   Total Profit = 400 x 55 - Total cost
            = 22000 – 20065.725
   Total profit = 1934.275 Rs.

Example: 5 used rivets at an approximate constant rate of 5000 kg /year.
The rivet cost Rs.20/- per kg and company personal estimate that it cost 200/- Rs. To place an order. The carrying cost of inventory is 10% per year of investment in the inventory.

i.   How frequently should the orders for rivet be placed?

ii.   What quantity should be order?

iii.   What is minimum yearly total cost?

Given,
Annual requirement   = 9000 parts/year

∴ q= $\dfrac{9000}{12}$ = 750 parts/month

C = 20 part
Co = Ordering Cost = 15/order

Ch = Carrying Charges = $20 \times \dfrac{15}{100}$ = 3 parts/year
= 15%

Total annual variable cost

$$= \frac{q}{2}.Ch + \frac{R}{q} Co$$

$$= Rs \left[\frac{750}{2}.3 + \frac{9000}{750}.15\right]$$

$$= Rs.1305$$

EoQ in unit

$$Q_o = \sqrt{\frac{2R.Co}{.Ch}} = \sqrt{\frac{2 \times 9000 \times 15}{3}}$$

$$= 300 \text{ Units}$$

Total annual variable cost

$$= \sqrt{2.R.Ch.Co}$$
$$= \sqrt{2 \times 9000 \times 3 \times 15}$$
$$= 900 \text{ Rs.}$$

No of orders

$$N = \sqrt{\frac{R.Ch}{2.Co}}$$

$$= \sqrt{\frac{9000.3}{2.15}}$$

$$= \sqrt{900}$$

$$N = 30 \text{ order/year.}$$

Hence, if the company purchase , 300 units each time and places 30 orders in the year, the net saving to the company will be (1305 – 900) 405/- Rs. Per year.

Exercise

A manufacturing company purchase 9000 parts cf a machine for its annual requirements, ordering on month wage at time. Each parts cost Rs. 20/-
The ordering cost per order is Rs.15/- and the carrying charges are 15% of the average inventory per year
Find
1. EOQ

2. TVE

3. N

Hint
You have been asked to suggest a more economical purchasing policy for the company. What advice would you offer and how much would it save the company per year?

Chapter VI

Replacement Model

Introduction : As the system becomes older its repair and maintenance cost increases and with the passage cf time it become mode economic to replace an old equipment by a new one.
But a clear-cut time for replacement is very difficult to define. However it is possible to define a replacement policy. The

replacement policy, in this case, consist of calculating the increased operating cost, maintenance cost ,forced idle time cost together with cost of replacing the new equipment.

There are another type of problem, invokes the replacement of item such as replacement of bulb, radio tube etc. of equipment which does not deteriorate with time but suddenly fails. Here the problem is of finding which items to replace and when to replace, and finding it we can replace them in a group.

There is yet another class of equipment which becomes obsolete, due to new discoveries and Technological advancement.

∴= > Replacement is not necessary due to reduced efficiency or standard,but it is necessary due to technological development for standard hugeness.

For each category of item mentioned above, different policies(models)for replacement have to be developed that are called replacement models

Replacement Model/Types of Models :

I.   Replacement of items that Deteriorate.(i.e whose maintenance cost increase with Time ignoring changes in the value of money during the period)

II.   Replacement of items whose maintenance cost increase with time and value of money also changes with time.

III.   Replacement of items that fail suddenly(Group Replacement Policy).

*1)   Replacement of items whose maintenance and repair cost increase with time, ignoring   changes in the value of money during the period .

Let us consider a simple situation which consist of minimizing the average annual cost of an equipment, whose maintenance cost is function increasing with time and whose scrap value is constant .

As the time value of money is not to be considered, the interest rate is zero and the calculation can be based in average annual cost.

C: capital cost of the item / equipment .

S: scrap value of the item.

Tavg: Average annual total cost of the item.

n: Number of year the item is to be in use .

f(t): Operating & maintenance cost of the item at time 't'.

Case 1: When time 't' is cotineous variable.
Annual cost if the items at any time 't'= Capital cost – scrap value + maintenance cost.

Total cost incurred during 'n' years T(n)=C – S + $\int_0^\infty f(t).dt$

Total maintenance cost incurred during 'n' years = $\int_0^\infty f(t).dt$
∴ Average annual cost incurredon the item Tare=

$\frac{1}{n}\left| C - S + \int_0^\infty f(t).dt \right|$

Note :=> Equipment / Items should be replaced when maintenance cost equals the average annual cost when 't' is contineous variable.
Case 2: When time 't' is a discreate variable.

Total cost incurred during 'n' years | T(n)=C – S + $\sum_{t=0}^{n} f(t)$

∴ Average annual cost incurred during 'n' years = f(n) =
$\frac{1}{n}[C - S + \sum_{t=0}^{n} f(t)]$

Note :=> When 't' is a discrete variable and next year running cost is more than average cost of the previous year ($n^{th}\,year$) then it is economical to replace it art the end of $n^{th}\,year$. And if the present year's running cost is less than the previous year's average cost, then donot replace.

Examples :=>
1) The cost of machine is Rs 6100 /- and its scrap value is Rs 100. The maintenance cost found from experience are as follow.

Year	1	2	3	4	5	6	7	8
Maintenance	100	250	400	600	900	1200	1600	2000

Find when should the machine be replaced ?

→ Let,

It be profitable to replace the machine after 'n' years.

Then 'n' is determined by the minimum value of the Tare.

Value of Tare for various year are calculated in the table as.

(1)	(2)	(3)	(4)	(5)	(6)
Years of service (n)	Purchase Price scrap value $[C - S]$	Annual maintenance cost $f(t)$	Summation of maintenance cost $\sum_{t=0}^{n} f(t)$	Total cost $T(n) = C - S + \sum_{t=0}^{n} f(t)$	Average annual cost $= \text{Tare } \frac{1}{n} [C - S + \sum_{t=0}^{n} f(t)]$
	Rs	Rs	Rs	Rs	Rs
1	6000	100	100	6100	6100
2	6000	250	350	6350	3175
3	6000	400	750	6750	2250
4	6000	600	1350	7350	1837.50
5	6000	900	2250	8250	1650
6	6000	1200	3450	9450	1575
7	6000	1600	5050	11050	1578

8	6000	2000	7050	13050	1631

∴ Table shows that .

The average annual cost is minimum (Rs 1575) during the sixth year and then rises.

Hence , machine should be replaced after 6 years of its use.

2) The maintenance cost and resale value per year of a machine whose purchase price is Rs 7000 /- is given below .

Year	1	2	3	4	5	6	7	8
Mainten ance Cost in (Rs).	900	1200	1600	2100	2800	3700	4700	5900
Resale value in (Rs).	4000	2000	1200	600	500	400	400	400

When should the machine be replaced ?

→ ∴ Capital cost c=Rs.7000 and it be profitable to replace the machine after 'n' year. Then 'n' should be determined by the minimum value of Targ.

Targ for various years are computed in table below.

(1)	(2)	(3)	(4)	(5)	(6)	(7)
Year of service (n)	Resale value (s)	Purchase price −resale value.	Annual maintenance cost f(t).	Summation of maintenance cost $\sum_{t=0}^{n} f(t)$	Total cost C − S + $\sum_{t=0}^{n} f(t)$	Average annual cost $\frac{1}{n}$[C − S + $\sum_{t=0}^{n} f(t)$]
1	4000	3000	900	900	3900	3900
2	2000	6000	1200	2100	7100	3550
3	1200	5800	1600	3700	9500	3166.67
4	600	6400	2100	5800	12200	3050
5	500	6500	2800	8600	15100	3020
6	400	6600	3700	12300	18900	3150
7	400	6600	4700	17000	23600	3371.43
8	400	6600	5900	22900	29500	3687.50

Hence , we observe that average annual cost is minimum(Rs.3020) in 5th year .
∴ Machine should fbe replaced at the end of 5 years of service.

3) The purchase price of a machine is Rs.52000. The installation charges amount to Rs.14400 and its scrap value is only Rs.6400. The maintenance cost in various years is given below.

Year	1	2	3	4	5	6	7	8
Maintenance cost	1000	3000	4000	6000	8400	11600	1600	19200

How many years should the machine be replaced ?.
→ Assume that the machine replacement can be done only at the years ends.
Cost of machine C=Rs.(52000+14400)=Rs.66400/-
Scrap value S=Rs.6400 /-

(1)	(2)	(3)	(4)	(5)	(6)
Years of service (n)	Purchase Price resale value [C − S]	Annual maintenance cost $f(t)$	Summation of maintenance cost $\sum\limits_{t=0}^{n} f(t)$	Total cost $T(n)= C - S + \sum\limits_{t=0}^{n} f(t)$	Average annual cost $=\text{Tare } \frac{1}{n} [C - S + \sum\limits_{t=0}^{n} f(t)]$
1	60000	1000	1000	61000	61000
2	60000	3000	4000		
3	60000	4000	8000	64000	32000
4	60000	6000	14000	68000	22667
5	60000	8400		68000	22667
6	60000	11600	22400	74000	18500
7	60000	16000	34000		
8	60000	19200		82400	16480
			50000	94000	15667
			69200	110000	157

				0	00	14
					1292 00	161 50

Hence, we observe that average annual cost will increase at the end of 6 years , hence machine should be replaced at the end of 6 years of service.

*2).Replacement of itms whose maintenance cost increase with time and value of money also change with time.
*As the value of money changes with time we must calculate the present value / worth value to be spent over a few years (denoted by V).
* If it is interest rate then it is considered as rate of inflation (sum of rate of interest and inflation) per year (denoted by i)

∴ Rupee invested at present $= (1+i)^1$ for present year
∴ Rupee invested for two years $= (1+i)^2$
∴ Rupee invested for n^{th} years $= (1+i)^n$
∴ Present value / worth value spent after n^{th} year $= (1+i)^{-n}$

$$V = \frac{1}{(1+i)^n} \quad \text{is}$$

called discount rate.

∴ Present value for 1st year $V = \dfrac{1}{(1+i)^1}$

∴ Present value for 2nd year $V = \dfrac{1}{(1+i)^2}$

∴ Present value for 3rd year $V = \dfrac{1}{(1+i)^3}$

∴ Present value for n^{th} year $V = \dfrac{1}{(1+i)^n}$

Examples :-

1) The yearly cost of two machine A and B when money value is neglected is shown in table. Find their cost patterns if maney value is 10 % per years and hence find which machine is more economical.

Year	1	2	3
Machine A (Rs).	1800	1200	1400

Machine B (Rs).	2800	200	1400

=> We know that ,

Per year discount cost = Per year total cost $\times$ V^{r-1}

∴ Total expenditure for each machine in there years when money value are considered is Rs. 4400.

∴ Both the machine are equals good, but when the value of money is 10 % per year, the discount rate $V = \dfrac{1}{1+0.10}$

$= \dfrac{1}{1.1} = 0.9090$ /-

∴ The discount cost pattern for machine A and B are

	(1) V^{r-1}	(2)	(3)	(4) Total cost (Rs)
Year machine 'A' (Discounted cost in Rs)	1800	=1200 x 0.9091 =1090.90	=1400 x 0.9091 =1157.04	=4047.94
Year machine 'B' (Discounted cost in Rs)	2800	=200 x 0.9091 =181.82	=1400 x 0.9091 =1157.04	=4138.86

∴ => Total cost of machine 'B' is greater than total cost of machine 'A' .

∴ Machine A is more economical than machine 'B'.

2) A machine cost Rs. 500 operation and maintenance cost is zero for the first year and increase by Rs 100 every year. If money is worth 5 % every year. Determine the best age at which the machine should be replaced. The resale value of the machine is negligibly small. What is the weighted average cost of owning and operating the machine?

=> Given that ,
Machine cost Rs.500. and money is worth 5 % every year.

$$\therefore \text{ Discount rate } V = \frac{1}{1+r} = \frac{1}{1+0.05} = 0.9524 \text{ /-}$$

The best replacement year for machine is find in the table.

(1)	(2)	(3)	(4)	(5)	(6)	(7)
Years of service (n)	Maintenance cost	Discount Factor (V^{r-1})	Discount cost ($R_r V^{r-1}$)	$C + \sum\limits_{r=1}^{n} R_r V^r$	$\sum\limits_{r=1}^{n} V^{r-1}$	$\dfrac{C + \sum\limits_{r=1}^{n} R_r V^{r-1}}{\sum\limits_{r=1}^{n} V^{r-1}}$
1	0	1.000	0.00	500.00	1.0000	1.000
2	100	0.9524	95.24	595.24	1.9524	1.9524
3	200	0.9070	181.40	776.64	2.8594	24
4	300	0.8638	259.14	1035.78	3.7232	2.8594
5	400	0.8227	329.08	1364.86	4.5459	3.7232
						4.5459

$\therefore \Rightarrow$ Machine should be replaced at the end of 3 rd years .
These after replacement cost will increase.

3) A manufacturer is offered two machines A and B . A has cost price of Rs. 2500, its running cost is Rss.400 for each of the first 5 years and increases by Rs. 100 every subsequent year. Machine 'B' , having the same capacity as A. cost Rs.1250 has running cost of Rs.600 per 6 years, increasing be Rs.100 per year thereafter. If money is worth 10 % per

year which machine should be purchased . Scrap value of both machines is nigligibally small.

=>
As money is worth 10 % per year , the discount rate for both machine is

$$V = \frac{1}{1+r} = \frac{1}{1+0.10} = 0.9091 \text{ /-}$$

Separate calculation for machine A and machine B are entered in table.

Machine – A

(1) Years of service (n)	(2) Maintenance cost	(3) Discount Factor (V^{r-1})	(4) Discount cost ($R_r V^{r-1}$)	(5) $C + \sum_{r=1}^{n} R_r V^{r-1}$	(6) $\sum_{r=1}^{n} V^{r-1}$	(7) $\frac{(5)}{(6)}$
1	400	1.000	400.00	2900.00	1000.0	2900.00
2	400	0.9091	363.24	3263.64	1.9091	1709.45
3	400	0.8264	330.56	3594.20	2.7355	1313.84
4	400	0.7513	300.52	3894.72	3.4868	1116.93
5	400	0.6830	273.20	4167.92	4.1698	999.50
6	500	0.6209	31447	447	4.7	934
7	600	0.5645				
8	700	0.5132				
9	800	0.4665				
10	900	0.4241				

(4)	(5)	(6)	(7)
0.45	8.37	90 7	.80 899
33 8.7 0	481 7.0 7	5.3 55 2	.40 881 .92
35 9.2 4	517 6.3 1	5.8 68 4	875 .86
37 3.2 0	554 9.5 1	6.3 34 9	877 .35
38 1.6 9	593 1.2 0	6.7 59 0	

From the above table we conclude that for machine A cost will increase after 9 th year .

∴ Machine should be replaced before the end of 9 th year._____ (a)

Machine – B

(1)	(2)	(3)	(4)	(5)	(6)	(7)
Years of service (n)	Maintenance cost	Discount Factor (V^{r-1})	Discount cost ($R_r V^{r-1}$)	$C + \sum\limits_{r=1}^{n} R_r V^{r-1}$	$\sum\limits_{r=1}^{n} V^{r-1}$	$\dfrac{(5)}{(6)}$
1	600	1.000	60 0.0 0	185 0.0 0	10 00 0	185 0.0 0
2	600	0.909 1	54 5.4 6	239 5.4 6	1.9 09 1	125 4.7 5
3	600	0.826 4				
4	600	0.751	49 5.8	289 1.3	2.7 35	105 6.9
5	600					

6	600	3	4	0	5	5
7	700	0.6830	450.78	3342.08	3.4868	958.49
8	800	0.6209	409.80	3751.88	4.1698	899.77
9	900	0.5645	372.54	4124.42	4.7907	860.92
10	1000	0.5132	395.15	4519.57	5.3552	843.96
		0.4665	410.56	4930.13	5.8684	840.11
		0.4241	419.85	5349.98	6.3349	844.52
			424.10	5774.08	6.7590	854.28

∴ Table (2) indicates that machine (B) cost will increase after the end of 8 th year _____(b)

∴ From (a) and (b) it indicates that machine (B) is more economical than machine (A).

∴ It is advisible to purchase machine (B).

*(3) Replacement of Items that fails suddenly

A system usually consist of a large number of low cost items that are increasingly liable to fail with age [e.g. failure of some resister in radio, TV computer etc] also failure of tub lights , bulbs etc.

failure of pumps (industrial equipment) in a refinery may close down entire system.
*Two types of replacement policies are considered when dealing with such situations.
1) Individual replacement policy.
2) Group replacement policy.
** Group replacement policy
Quit oftem a system consist of a large number of identical, low cost items which are more and more likely to fail with time .
If may be economical to replace all such items at fixed intervals.
Such a policy is called group replacement policy and is particularly sutaible when cost of individual item is comparatively small.
e.g. Replacement of street light bulbs.
Thus under this policy use replace all the items at a fixed interval 't' , wheather they here failed or not .
The problem is to determine optimul group replacement time interval.
N= Total no. of items in the system
Nt = No. of items that fail during time 't'.
C (t) = The total cost of group replacement after a time 't'.

Average cost per unit is = $\frac{C\ (t)}{t}$

Examples :-
   1) Find the cost per period of individual replacement policy of an installation of 300 bulbls.
      Given the following .

      I.   Cost of replacing individual bulb is Rs.2
      II. Conditional probability of falure is given below

Week No conditional	0	1	2	3	4
Probablity of failure	0	0.1	0.3	0.7	1.0

Also, find / calculate no. of light bulbs that would fail during the each of four week.
   ⇨ Let, Pi be the probably that alight bulb fails during the ith week of its life then

   $\{$ Po=0   P3= 0.7 - 0.3 =0.4

P1= 0.1   P4= 1.0 – 0.7
=0.3

P2= 0.3 - 0.1= 0.2

Since we know,
Sum of all the above probabilities is unity .
∴ =>probability after(after P4) 5 week = zero.

∴ => all the light bulbls are sure to burn out by the 4th week.

Let Ni represent the no. of replacement mode at the end of ith week , when all the 300 bulbs are new initially then.

We have,

Week	Expected No. of failure	
0	No	=300
1	N1= NoP1 = 300 x 0.1= 30	
2	N2= NoP2 + N1P1 + NoPo	
	=(300x0.2) + (30x0.1) + 0 (∵ Po=0)	
	= 60 + 3 = 63	
3	N3= NoP3 + N1P2 + N2P1 + N3P0	
	=(300x0.4) + (30x0.2) + (63x0.1) + (N3x0)	
	= 132	
4	N4=NoP4 + N1P3 + N2P2 + N3P1 + N4Po	
	=(300x0.3) + (30x0.4) + (63x0.2) + (132x0.1) + (N4x0)	
	= 128	

∴ =>no. of light bulbs fails during the week 1,2,3 and 4 are 30,63,132 and 128 respectively.

Also,
We find that no. of bulbs failing each week increases till end n 3rd week and then decreases during the 4th week.

∴ Average life of light bulbs = $\sum\limits_{i=1}^{4} i$ Pi
= (1x0.1) + (2x0.2) + (3x0.4) + (4x0.3)

=2.9 weeks

Average no. of failure per week = $\dfrac{Total\ no.of\ bulbs}{Avg.life\ of\ bulb}$

= $\dfrac{300}{2.9}$

= 103 (approx)

Also,
Cost of individual replacement of bulbs = Rs.2 x 103
= Rs. 206 / week

2) The following mortality rates have been observed for a retain type of light bulbs in an installation with 1000 bulbs .

End of week	1	2	3	4	5	6
Probably of failure to date	0.9	0.25	0.49	0.85	0.97	1.00

There are large no. of such a bulbs which are to be kept in a working order. If bulbs fails in service , it costs Rs.3 to replace but if all bulbs are replaced in the same operation , it can be done for only Rs.0.70 a bulb . It is proposed to replace all bulbs at fixed intervals, wheather or not they have burn out, and to continue replacing burnt out bulbs as they fail
a) What is the best interval between group replacement .
b) Also establishe if the policy , as determined by you , is superior to the policy of replacing bulbs as and when they fail , there being nothing like group replacement .
c) At what group replacement price per bulb , would a policy of strictly individual replacement become preferable to the adopted policy.
⇨ Let, assume that

Pi be the probability that as light bulbs fails during the ith week of its life then.

$P_1 = 0.09$

$P_2 = 0.25 - 0.09$ =0.16

$P_3 = 0.49 - 0.25$ = 0.24

$P_4 = 0.85 - 0.49$ = 0.36

$P_5 = 0.97 - 0.85$ = 0.12

$P_6 = 1.00 - 0.97$ = 0.03

=>Total of all probablin = 1
=>P_7, P_8,--------------------etc=0.
=>Thus all the light bulbs are sure to burn out be the end of 6th week.

Let, Ni represent the no of replacement made at the end of ith week , when all the 1000 bulbs are new initially then .

Week (i)	Expected No. of failure (Ni).
0	$N_0 = N_0$ =1000
1	$N_1 = N_0 P_1$ = 1000 x 0.09 =90
2	$N_2 = N_0 P_2 + N_1 P_1$ =(1000 x 0.16) + (90 x 0.09) =168
3	$N_3 = N_0 P_3 + N_1 P_2 + N_2 P_1$ = (1000 x 0.24) + (90 x 0.16) + (168 x 0.09) =269
4	$N_4 = N_0 P_4 + N_1 P_3 + N_2 P_2 + N_3 P_1$ = (1000 x 0.36) + (90 x 0.24) + (168 x 0.16) +(269 x 0.09) =432
5	$N_5 = N_0 P_5 + N_1 P_4 + N_2 P_3 + N_3 P_2 + N_4 P_1$

	$=(1000 \times 0.12) + (90 \times 0.36) + (168 \times 0.24) +$ $(269 \times 0.16) + (432 \times \ 0.09)$ $=274$
6	$N_6 = N_0 P_6 + N_1 P_5 + N_2 P_4 + N_3 P_3 + N_4 P_2 + N_5 P_1$ $=(1000 \times 0.03) + (90 \times 0.12) + (168 \times 0.36)$ $+(269 \ \times \ 0.24) + (432 \times 0.16) + (274 \times 0.09)$ $=260$
7	$N_7 = 0 + N_1 P_6 + N_2 P_5 + N_3 P_4 + N_4 P_3 + N_5 P_2 + N_6 P_1$ $= (0) + (90 \times 0.03) + (168 \times 0.12) + (269 \times 0.36)$ $+ (432 \times 0.24) + (274 \times 0.16) \ + (260 \times 0.09)$ $=291$

=>No. of bulbs falling each week increase till the end of 4th week , then decreases and again increases from 7th week.
Now we can determine the total and , there by , the average weekly cost associated with the policy of replacing bulbs every week , every two weeks----------- and so on.
As per group replacement policy replacement of all bulbs as a same time after fixed interval , operation cost is Rs. 0.70 per bulb and individual replacement cost Rs.3 /- per bulbs.
  a) Determination of optimal group replacement interval.

Upto the week	Total cost of group replacement (Rs).	Aveg. Cost per week (Rs).
1	1000 x 0.70 + 90 x 3 = 970	970.00
2	1000 x 0.70 + 3 (90 + 168) = 1474	737.00--------(b)
3	1000 x 0.70 + 3 (90 + 168 + 269) = 2281	760.33

=>Average minimum cost is in the 2nd week .

∴ It is optimal to have group replacement after every two weeks.

b) To find individual replacement cost for that find .

Average (expected) life of the light bulbs $= \sum_{i=1}^{6} iPi$

= (1 x 0.09) + (2 x 0.16) + (3 x 0.24) + (4 x 0.36)   +(5 X 0.12) + (6 X 0.03)=3.35

Then find ,

Average number of failure per week $= \frac{Total\ no.of\ bulbs}{Avg.life\ of\ bulbs}$

$= \frac{1000}{3.35}$ = 299

∴   Cost of individual replacement of bulb per week
=Avg. no. of failure per week × individual replacement price of bul
=299 × 3
=Rs.897 /-----------------------(b)

∴   From (a) and (b) it indicates that cost of group replacement = 737.00/- Per week.

& cost of individual replacement = 897.00/- Per week.

=>It is advisable to adopt the policy of group replacement .

c) Let Rs. 'x' be the group replacement price per bulb then

Rs. 897 < $\dfrac{1000(x)+3(90+168)}{2}$

$\therefore \Rightarrow x > Rs.1.02$

=>When the group replacement price per bulb exceed Rs.1.02, then the policy of strictly individual replacement becomes more economical.

Chapter VII

Queuing Theory

Characteristics of queuing phenomenon:

Queuing theory or waiting line are familiar phenomena, which we observe quite frequently in our daily life.

- The characteristics of queuing phenomenon are,

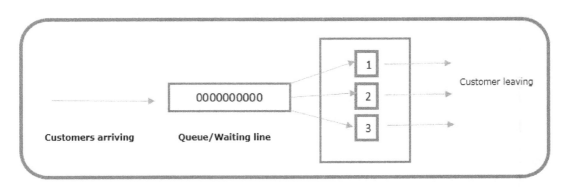

Customers arriving   Queue/Waiting line

i) Units arrives at regular or irregular interval of time to the given point called as service center

Example

Trucks arriving a loading stations customer entering to a department store persons arriving a cinema hall.
All these units are called entries or arrivals of customer.

ii) One or more service channels or service states or service facilities (ticket window, sales girl, typist are assembled at the service center

If service station is empty, arriving customer will be served immediately.

If not, the arriving customer will wait in line until the service is provided.

Once service is provided, customer leaves the system.

The major constituents of a queuing system are

i) Customer :

The arriving unit that requires some service to be performed.
The customer may be person, m/c, vehicles, parts.

ii) Queue (Waiting line) :

The number of customers waiting to be service. The queue **does not** include the customer(s) being serviced.

iii) Service channel :

The process of the facility which is performing the service to the customer.

This may be **single** or **Multi-channel**.

Elements of Queuing System. (Structure of queuing system) :

A queuing system is specified completely by seven main element.

1) Input or arrival distribution

2) Output or departure (service) distribution

3) Service channel

4) Service discipline

5) Maximum number of customer allowed in the system.

6) Calling source or population

7) Customer's behavior

1. Arrival Distribution :

It represents the pattern in which the number of customers arrives at the service facility. Arrivals may also be represented by the **inter-arrival time,** which is the period between two successive arrivals.

Arrivals may be separated by equal **interval** of time or by unequal but definitely known intervals of time or unequal interval i.e. **random.**

The rate at which customers arriving per unit of time is called as **'arrival rate'.**

When the arrival rate is random, the customer arrives in no logical pattern or order over time. Random arrivals are best described by **'Poison distribution.'**

Mean value of arrival rate is represented by ' λ '

2. <u>Service (Departure) distribution :</u>

It represents the pattern in which the number of customers gets the service facility (center). Departure may also be represented by the service time which is the time period between two success and services.

Service time may be constant or variable but known or random. Random service time is best described by **exponential probability distribution.**

The rate at which one service channel can perform the service i.e. number of customer served per unit of time is called **'Service rate.'**

Means value of service rate is represented by 'μ'

3. <u>Service Channel :</u>

A queuing model is called as **'One Server model'** when the system has one server only **'Multi server modes'** when the system has a number of parallel channels each with one server.

A queuing system has a **single service channel**. So, arriving customers may form one line and get serviced e.g. Doctor's clinic.

The system may have a **number of service channels**, which may be arranged in parallel or in series or complex combination of both.

So, several customer may service simultaneous e.g. In barber shop.

For **series channel**, a customer must pass successively through all the channel before service is completed.

4. **Service Discipline :**

It is the order of service. The rule by which customers are selected from the queue for service.

FCFS: First Come First Serve.

It is the most common discipline. According to it, customers are served in order of their arrival. For example. railway station, bank.

LCFS: Last Come First Serve

As in a big godown, where the items arriving last are taken out first.

Random Order: Any Order

Priority: When arriving customer is chosen for service ahead of some other services in queue.

5. **Maximum number of customers allowed in the system.**

It can be either finite or infinite. In some facilities, only limited numbers of customers are allowed in the system and new arriving customers are not allowed to join the system unless the number becomes less than the limited value.

6. **Calling source or population :**

The arrival pattern of the customers depends on the source which generates them.

If there are only a few potential customers the calling source (population) is called as finite.

If there are large number of potential customer (more than 40 to 50), it is usually said to be infinite.

7. **Customer's behavior :**

If a customer decides not to enter the queue, since it is too long, he is said to have **'balked.'**

If customer enters the queue, but after sometime loses patience and leaves it, he is said to be **'reneged.'**

When there are 2 or more queue parallel, the customer move from one queue to another, they are said to be **'jockeying.'**

IMP Formulas:

λ =   mean arrival rate per unit time   or Average arrival rate

μ =   Average service rate per unit time

μ $>$ λ

Ws   =   Average waiting time of customer in System

Ws=Avg Waiting Time of customer in Queue $$\dfrac{1}{\mathbf{w_s}\mu \ -\lambda}$$	Probe that there are n or more cust present in System. $$[\mathbf{Pn}=Po(\tfrac{\lambda}{\mu})^n] =(1-\tfrac{\lambda}{\mu})\,(\tfrac{\lambda}{\mu}^n)$$
Wq=Avg waiting time of customer in Queue $$Wq=\dfrac{\lambda}{\mu\,(\mu -\lambda)}$$	Proba that customer has to wait more cust present in Queue. $$Pk = (\dfrac{\lambda}{\mu})_k$$
Ls=Avg.no.of Customer in system length $$\mathbf{Ls}=\dfrac{\lambda}{\mu -\lambda}$$	Proba that customer has to wait more. $$e^{-(\mu -\lambda)t}$$ e=2.718
Lq=Avg.no of Customer in Queue $$\mathbf{Lq}=\dfrac{\lambda^2}{\mu\,(\mu -\lambda)}$$	Proba that customer has to wait more time in queue. $$\dfrac{\lambda}{\mu}\,e^{-(\mu-\lambda)t}$$

It is Utilization Factor System Is Busy ,It's Utilization is Going on. $$\varphi= \frac{\lambda}{\mu}$$	Avg Length of Queue the Forms From Time To Time. $$Lb= \frac{\mu}{\mu-\lambda}$$
It Show System is empty .System is not busy. Utilization of sys is off. $$Lb=1- -\frac{\lambda}{\mu}$$	

Waiting Line Theory / Queuing Theory

Characteristics of queue model

Queuing system consist of arrival unit (customer m/c, clients, raw material) waiting for the service & their departure from the system.

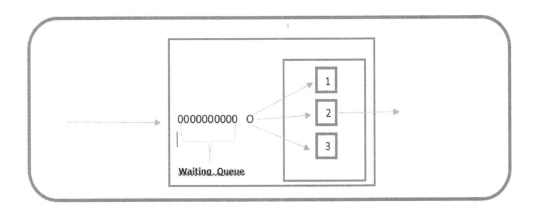

Mode of Queuing system.

Notations:

λ   =   Mean arrival rate per unit time. Average arrival rate
per unit   time

μ   =   Average service rate per unit time

Ws   =   Waiting average time of customer in system

$$W_s = \left(\frac{1}{}\right.$$

Wq   =   Average waiting time of a customer

                        In the queue only.

Ls   =   Average number of customer in system

$$Ls = \frac{\lambda}{\mu - \lambda}$$

Lq   =   Average number of customer waiting in queue

$$Lq = \frac{\lambda^2}{\mu(\mu - \lambda)}$$

$\Phi = \dfrac{\lambda}{\mu}$ it is utilization factor.

That means system is busy and it's utilization is going on.

$P0 = 1 - \dfrac{\lambda}{\mu}$

It means Probability that system is empty.

Utilization of system is off system is not busy.

1. **Elements of queuing modes :**

    i)   **Arrival pattern:**

        Arrival per unit time is called as arrival rate.

    ii)   **Service pattern :**

        Service per unit time is called as service rate. (μ)

        Poison distribution for non-probability

        Exponential rate

iii)   **Service channel :**

        Single channel (e.g. 1 clerk, 1 cashier)

        Multi channel

        XXXXXX

iv)   **Service discipline :**

        FCFS, LCFS, Random(interview), Priority (urgency)

v)   Maximum number of people allowed in system

vi)   Calling source / population

Q.   A departmental store has single cashier. The number of customer arriving 20 per hour. Cashier takes 2.5 min. on an average to gives service to a customer.
Assume that arrival rate follows poison distribution and service rate follows exponential distribution.

Find:

    I)   Probability, of cashier is busy.

    ii)   Average waiting time of customer to get service.

    iii)   Average number of customer waiting for service.

Given:

-   Mean arrival rate (   ) = 20 cost / hr.

-   Mean service rate (μ) = 2.5 / per min   - 1 cost

    Therefore μ =   24 cost/hr   (0) 5 min - 2 cost

i.e.   (0) 10 min – 4 cost

                             (0) 60 min – 24 cost

i)   Probability that cashier is busy :

i.e. Server utilization going on

$$\varphi = \frac{\lambda}{\mu}$$

$$= \frac{20}{24}$$

$$\Phi = 0.83$$

= 83% cashier is busy.

ii)   Average **waiting** time of customer to get **service.**

Customer in queue.

$$Wq = \frac{\lambda}{\mu\,(\mu - \lambda)}$$

$$= \frac{20}{24\,(24 - 20)}$$

$$= \frac{20}{24 * 4}$$

$$= \frac{20}{96}$$

= 0.209 per hour

= 17 min

iii)   Average number of customer waiting for service in queue.

$$Lq= \frac{\lambda^2}{\mu\,(\mu - \lambda)}$$

$$= \frac{20}{24\,(24 - 20)}$$

$$= \frac{20}{24 * 4}$$

$$= \frac{100}{24}$$

$$= 4.1$$

Q.   Customer arrives at window drive according to poison distribution, with a mean of 10 min. and service time per customer is exponential with a mean of 6 min. The space in front of window can accommodate only 3 vehicles including the service 1.

Other vehicles have to wait outside this space.

Calculate,

    i)   Probability, that arriving customer can drive directly to the space in front of window.

ii)	Probability, that arriving customer will have to wait outside the directed space.

iii)	How long an arriving customer is expected to wait before getting the service?

Important Formula

Probability that there are n or more customer present in the system.

Probability that there are XXX or more people / customer present in queue. Probability, that customer has to wait more XXXX min in the system. In the queue

i)	Probability that an arriving customers can directly drive in front of window.

Total Formula= P0+p1+p2

$$=(1-\frac{\lambda}{\mu})+ P0.(\frac{\lambda}{\mu})^1+P0.(\frac{\lambda}{\mu})^2$$

$$=(1-\frac{\lambda}{\mu})+(1-\frac{\lambda}{\mu}).(\frac{\lambda}{\mu})+(1-\frac{\lambda}{\mu})+.(\frac{\lambda}{\mu})^2$$

$$=[1-\frac{\lambda}{\mu}].[1+(1-\frac{\lambda}{\mu})^1+(\frac{\lambda}{\mu})^2]$$

$$=(1-\frac{6}{10}).[1+(\frac{6}{10})+(\frac{36}{100})]$$

$$=(\frac{4}{10}).(\frac{100+60+36}{100})$$

$$= \left(\frac{4}{10}\right) . \left(\frac{196}{100}\right)$$

$$= \frac{784}{1000}$$

$$= 0.784$$

ii)   Probability of arriving customer will wait at outside the directed space.

$$= 1 - 0.784$$

$$= 0.216$$

$$= 21\%$$

iii)   How long an arriving customer is expected to wait before getting service,

$$Wq = \frac{\lambda}{\mu \, (\mu \, - \, \lambda)}$$

$$= \frac{6}{10 \, (10 \, - \, 6)}$$

$$= \frac{6}{40}$$

$$= 0.15 \, / \, hrs$$

$$= 0.15 * 60 \, min$$

$$= 9 \, min$$

Q.   Assume that at bank teller window the customer arrive at the average rate of 20 per hours accordingly to poison distribution.

Assume that bank teller spends average of 2 min per customer to complete a service and service time is exponentially distributed. Customers are served on FCFS basis.

Find,

i) What is expected waiting time in the system?

ii) Mean number of customer waiting in system.

iii) What is probability of 'n' customer in system?

i) Expected time in the system.

λ = 20 /hrs.

μ = 2 min/hrs

i> Expected time in the system.

$$Ws = \cfrac{1}{\mu - \lambda}$$

$$= \cfrac{1}{30 - 20}$$

$$= \cfrac{1}{10}$$

$$= 0.1 \text{ hrs}$$

ii) Mean number of customer waiting in system.

$$Ls= \dfrac{\lambda}{\mu - \lambda}$$

$$= \dfrac{20}{10}$$

$$= 2 \text{ hrs.}$$

iii) Probability of 0 customers in system.

$$P0 = 1 - -\dfrac{\lambda}{\mu}$$

$$= 1 - -\dfrac{20}{30}$$

$$= 1 - 0.66$$

$$= 0.33$$

$$= 33\%$$

Q. In company the m/c that break down by following a poison process with average rate 4 per hour.

The m/c are then brought to repair section. Where only 1 repairman who provide services on contract.

The cost of non-productive m/c is 50 per hour. The repairman charges 100 Rs. Per hours and he repairs the m/c at an average rate of 6 hours.

Find,

i)   Average time for which a m/c will be kept in the repair shop.

ii)   Probability that there are at least 3 m/c in the repair shop.

iii)   Probability that a m/c will be kept in the queue for at least 15 min before it is repair.

λ=4 m/hrs.

μ=6 m/hrs.

i)

$$Ws = \frac{1}{\mu - \lambda}$$

$$= \frac{1}{6 - 4}$$

$$= \frac{1}{2}$$

= 0.5 hrs

=30 min

ii)   Probability that there are at least 3 m/c in repair shop

i.e. for service

$$P3 = (1\frac{\lambda}{\mu})^3$$

at least 3. 3 or more m/c atleast.

$$= (1\frac{\lambda}{\mu})(\frac{\lambda}{\mu})^3$$

$$= \frac{(1\frac{4}{6})}{(6)^3}\frac{4}{}$$

$$= \frac{(\frac{2}{6})}{(6)^3}\frac{4}{}$$

$$= (\frac{2}{6}) * \frac{64}{(216)}$$

$$= \frac{128}{1296}$$

$$= 0.098$$

iii)Probability that the m/c will in kept in the queue for at least 15 min before it is repair.

$$15 \text{ min} = \frac{1}{4} \text{ hrs.}$$

Proba that has to wait more time

T=1/4 hr in the queue.

$$P(t>=1/4) = \frac{\lambda}{\mu} \; e^{-(\mu-\lambda)t}$$

$$= \frac{\mu}{6} . e^{-(2)1/4}$$

$$= \frac{2}{3} . e^{-\lambda 2}$$

$$= \frac{2}{3} \cdot e^{-\lambda 2} \quad \text{where e=2.718}$$

$$= \frac{2}{3} \cdot (2.718)_{-1/2}$$

$$= \frac{2}{3} \frac{1}{\sqrt{2.718}}$$

$$= \frac{2}{3} \cdot \frac{1}{1.6486}$$

$$= \frac{2}{3} \cdot 0.609$$

$$= 1.2195/3$$

$$= 0.4065$$

Q) Arrivals at telephone booth are considered to be poison distribution with an average time of 10 min between arrival & the next.

The length of phone call is assumed to be distributed exponentially with mean 3 min.

i) What is probability that person arriving at the booth will have to wait.

ii) What is average length of the queue that forms time to time.

iii) What is probability that it will take him more than 10 min all together to wait for the phone and complete his call.

λ = 10 min =6 hrs.

μ=3 min   = 20 cust/hrs

Probability that system is busy or with utilization.

$$\Phi = \frac{\lambda}{\mu}$$

$$= \frac{6}{20}$$

$$= 0.3$$

$$=30\%$$

ii.   Average length of the queue that forms from time to time

$$Lb = \frac{\mu}{\mu - \lambda}$$

$$= \frac{20}{20 - 6}$$

$$= \frac{20}{14}$$

$$= 1.42$$

Approximately 1.42 cust forms from time to time.

iii)Probability that it will take him more than 10 min all together to wait phone.

More time t= $^{1}/_{6}$ hrs.

$$P(t>=\frac{\lambda}{\mu} e^{-(\mu-\lambda)t}$$

$$= \frac{6}{20} . e^{-(20-6)1/6}$$

$$= \frac{6}{20} . e^{-(14)/6}$$

$$=0.3 . (2.718)-7/3$$

$$=0.3 . \frac{1}{(2.718)7/3}$$

$$=0.029$$

Q. Self service store employs 1 cashier at the counter. 9 customers arrive on an average in every 5 minimum While the cashier can serve 10 customers in 5 min. Assuming poison distribution for arrival rate and exponential distribution for service time.

Find

      i)   Average number of customers in system

      ii)   Average queue length in queue

      iii)   Average time a customer spends in the system.

iv) Average time customer wait before being served.

v) Find probability that customer has to wait more 15 min. in the system.

1. A departmental store has a single cashier. During the rush hours, customers arrive as a rate of 20 customers per hour. The cashier takes on an average 2.5 min. per customer for processing.

Find

1) What is the probability that cashier is idle?

2) What is the average number of customers in the queuing system?

3) What is the average number of customers in the queuing system?

4) What is the average time spent by a customer in the system?

5) What is the average queue length?

6) What is the average time a customer spends in the queue waiting for the service?

Given that,

1) Customer arrival rate , λ = 20 per hour.

Cashier &customer take an avg 2.5 min to process 1 customer

$\Rightarrow$ μ =Avg Service rate per Unit time

$=\dfrac{60}{2.5}$ ->(min in hour).

μ=24 customer per hours.

Also λ>μ

2) Probability that cashier is idle = system is empty.

$$P0 = 1 - \frac{\lambda}{\mu}$$

$$= 1 - \frac{20}{24}$$

$$= 1 - \frac{5}{6}$$

$$= \frac{1}{6} \text{ or } 0.17.$$

3) Average number of customer in the queuing system = to fine average number of customer in the system.

$$Ls = \frac{\lambda}{\mu - \lambda}$$

$$= \frac{20}{24 - 20}$$

$$= \frac{20}{4}$$

$$= 5 \text{ customer.}$$

4) Average time spent by a customer in the system

i.e. average waiting time in the system is

$$Ws = \frac{1}{\mu - \lambda}$$

$$= \frac{1}{24 - 20}$$

$$= \frac{1}{4} \text{ hour}$$

$$= \frac{1}{4}(60)$$

$$= 15 \text{ min.}$$

5) What is average queue length

i.e. number find average number of customer in the queue.

$$Lq = \frac{\lambda^2}{\mu(\mu - \lambda)}$$

$$= \frac{(20)^2}{24(24 - 20)}$$

$$= \frac{20 * 20}{24 * 4}$$

$$= \frac{5 * 5}{6}$$

=4.17 cust

6) i.e.to find the

Average waiting time to customer in queue to get the system.

$$Wq = \frac{\lambda}{\mu(\mu - \lambda)}$$

$$= \frac{20}{24(24 - 20)}$$

$$= \frac{20}{24 * 4}$$

$$= \frac{5}{24} * 60$$

$$= 12.5 \text{ min}$$

Assume that at bank teller window the customer arrive at the average rate of 20 per hour according to Poisson distribution. Assume that bank teller spends average of 2 minutes per customer to complete a service and service time is exponentially distributed on FCIS basis.

Find

   i) What is the expected waiting time in the system?

   ii) Mean number of customer waiting in the system?

   iii) What is the probability of '0' customer in system?

Given that

  Arrival Rate λ= 20 per/hrs

  μ=2 min per Customer.

  μ=30 cust/hrs.

1) Expected waiting time in the system.

$$Ws= \frac{1}{\mu - \lambda}$$

$$= \frac{1}{30 - 20}$$

$$= \frac{1}{10}$$

$$=0.1$$

2)Mean number of customer waiting n the system.

 i.e to find avg no.of cust in the system length.

$$Ls= \frac{1}{\mu - \lambda}$$

$$= \frac{20}{30-20}$$

$$= \frac{20}{10}$$

=2 cust/hrs

3)Probability of '0' customer in the system.

i.e That is to find probability when system is empty.

$P0=1-\dfrac{\lambda}{\mu}$

$=1-\dfrac{20}{30}$

$=1-{}^{2}/_{3}$

$={}^{1}/_{3}$

$=0.33$

$P0=33\%$

(3)Customer arrives at window drive according to poison distribution, with a mean of 10 min and service time per customer is exponential with a mean of 6 min. The space in front of window can accommodate only 3 vehicle including the service 1 other vehicle have to wait outside two space.

Find

a) Probability that arriving customer can drive directly to the space in front of window.

b) Probability that arriving customer will have to wait outside the directed space.

c) How long an arriving customer is expected to wait before getting the service?

:   Total Probability is always = 1

Given that,

XXXXXX

Since, as initially there are 3 possibilities

     i)   When there are '0' vehicle present then probability = P_0

     ii)   When there are only '1' vehicle present then probability = P_1

     iii)   When there are only '2' vehicle present then probability = P_2

a) Probability that an arrive customer can drive directly to the space in front of window

Total Probability =

P0+p1+p2

$$=(1-\frac{\lambda}{\mu}) + P0.(\frac{\lambda}{\mu})^1 + P0.(\frac{\lambda}{\mu})^2$$

$$=(1-\frac{\lambda}{\mu})+(1-\frac{\lambda}{\mu}).(\frac{\lambda}{\mu})+(1-\frac{\lambda}{\mu})+ .(\frac{\lambda}{\mu})^2$$

$$= [1\tfrac{\lambda}{\mu}].[1+(1\tfrac{\lambda}{\mu})^1 + (\tfrac{\lambda}{\mu})^2]$$

$$=(1-\tfrac{6}{10}).[1+(\tfrac{6}{10})+(\tfrac{36}{100})]$$

$$=(\tfrac{4}{10}).(\tfrac{100+60+36}{100})$$

$$=(\tfrac{4}{10}).(\tfrac{196}{100})$$

$$=\tfrac{784}{1000}$$

$$=0.784$$

$$=78\%$$

b) Probability that arrived customer have to wait outside for directed space.

= 1-total prob where cust can drive directly to the space in Form of Window.

=1-0.784

=0.216

=21%

c) How long an arriving customer is expected to wait **before getting service** (i.e. in **queue**)

$$Wq= \frac{\lambda}{\mu\,(\mu - \lambda)}$$

$$= \frac{6}{10(10-6)}$$

$$= \frac{6}{40}$$

$$= 0.15 \text{ hrs}$$

$$= 0.15 * 60 \text{ min}$$

$$= 9 \text{ min}$$

www.ingramcontent.com/pod-product-compliance
Lightning Source LLC
Chambersburg PA
CBHW080408060326
40689CB00019B/4178